HOW BRIST

AND WILL KEEP ON WINNING

Bill Pezza

Author's Note and Acknowledgements

I had written three books prior to 2017, all works of historic fiction featuring heroic characters from Bristol Borough. They were well received in the area, and the experience was great fun. Anna's Boys was released in 2006, Stealing Tomatoes in 2009, and Homegrown in 2013. In recent years readers would often ask when my next book was coming out. My pat answer was that I had run out of ideas, and I doubted if there would ever be another.

Shortly after Bristol won the Small Business Revolution- Main Street contest sponsored by Deluxe Corporation from Shoreview, Minnesota, Harry Crohe asked the same question. When I gave him my standard answer, he replied that I should write about the SBR contest. Harry had been a workhorse in the process and felt people might enjoy a chronical of the experience for posterity.

The more I thought about Harry's idea, the more I felt that people like him, who had done so much for Bristol, deserved to have their story told. I decided to give it a shot and imposed a Labor Day deadline on myself so that the book would be released to coincide with the roll out of eight-part video series on the Bristol Borough/SBR experience. The series was to be aired on the Hulu cable network and on the Small Business Revolution website. That made for a busy summer, and I cursed Harry more than once during the effort, but I'm grateful for the nudge he gave me.

I suggest readers spend some time reviewing the **table of contents** carefully because you may enjoy the book by reading it cover to cover or by focusing only on the sections that interest you most.

I want to thank **Jean-Marc Dubus,** one of our gifted gallery artists at the Centre for the Arts, for his skillful cover design. In addition to his broad artistic interests, Jean-Marc is commissioned to create murals and hand painted signs. He can be reached at Marc@marcdubus.com.

I also want to thank **Kelly Sell** for her assistance with the formatting of this book. She bears no responsibility for its flaws, but deserves significant credit for its improvement.

Finally, I want to thank my wife and family for their support, advice and tolerance. Writing a book isn't always fun.

In HOW WE WON, I've done my best to acknowledge scores of people who played a vital role in the contest, but it is impossible to recognize everyone who contributed. I sincerely apologize to those I have missed.

Dedication

This book is dedicated to the hundreds, if not thousands of people who worked to advance Bristol Borough but are not mentioned here. You know who you are and you know what you did, and for that we are deeply grateful.

Raising the Bar
Board of Directors

Robin Butrey
Mycle Gorman
Ron McGuckin, Treasurer
Bill Pezza, President
Justin Saxton, Secretary
Joanna Schneyder, Vice President
Luke Wade
Ron Walker
Craig Whitaker

The Raising the Bar
Economic Development Sub-Committee

Don McCloskey, Joanna Schneyder, James Sell, Laura Wallick,
Donna Scalzo, Louis Quattrocchi, Tracy Timby, Ron Walker,
Bill Pezza, Craig Whitaker

Raising the Bar
Event Planners

Jose Acevido, Jimmy Bason, Daulton Brady, Shirley Brady, Ann
Kohn, Harry and Cathy Crohe, Stephanie Croquez, Lorraine and
Steve Cullen, Karen Dopson, Anna Larrisey, Bruce Lowe, Donna
McCloskey, Karen, Leighann, Greg & Dana Pezza, Jennifer
Renshaw, Joe Saxton, Dottie Saxton, Rich Schneyder, Robert
Strasser, Rose Marie Strippoli, Kelly Sell, Ronnie Walker,
Lynn Whitaker, and Carl White

Table of Contents

Introduction

Part III
Seed Planters:
"One Generation Plants the Seeds, Another Enjoys the Shade."

Quiet Heroes

Part IV
Game Changers

Introduction

Everyone loves an underdog. That time-worn statement still holds true, especially when referencing tiny Bristol Borough, in Bucks County, Pennsylvania. Like so many small, blue collar towns in America, this proud and once prosperous community fell on hard times when neighboring factories and mills closed or drastically reduced their workforce, resulting in a downward spiral of investment and diminished confidence in the town's future. But thanks to talented and effective local leaders, an incredible group of tenacious private volunteers and an amazing community spirit, the town clawed back from obscurity to emerge first out of 3,500 communities across America to win the national Small Business Revolution-Main Street contest (hereafter referred to as SBR), sponsored by Deluxe Corporation of Shoreview, Minnesota. Buoyed by its success, and bursting with renewed confidence, it stands poised to move forward, to create its own opportunities and to be a model of hope for other struggling towns whose best days CAN lie ahead.

This book is written for several reasons. First to celebrate and preserve for Bristol's residents and fans the wonderful story about one of their finest hours. Next, to recognize the individuals and groups that played such an important role in the victory. Third, to extend a challenge to the next generation of Bristolians to continue the significant work that needs to be done, mindful that *the day we stop moving forward is the day we start slipping backward.* And finally, to offer a blueprint and encouragement to other towns, that they can rise to new heights if they have a vision and empower their people.

Throughout this book I will reference scores of people who have led Bristol's charge over the past couple of decades, who laid the groundwork for our current success and who are working today to keep the momentum going. This is especially true of the civic group, Raising the Bar, of which I am proud to serve as president, and which spearheaded the SBR effort. Its core group of volunteers are remarkable people of vision, determination, and a selfless desire to serve. I also think **it's important to note that people like this exist in every struggling town in America. All they need is an opportunity to group, to organize and mobilize to reach their potential. Hopefully our story can be a catalyst to other towns making their own success stories.**

Speaking of a catalyst, we offer our undying gratitude to Deluxe Corporation for challenging us to step up. Their SBR mission to rebuild small town America one small business at a time is a noble one and their generosity and expertise will not be forgotten by the people of Bristol Borough.

When thinking about small towns across America, especially Historic Bristol Borough, I'm reminded of a Mark Twain story. Apparently, while Twain was traveling in London in the late 1890s, there were reports back home that he had died. Upon hearing the news, Twain, in satisfactory health, reportedly quipped, "The rumors of my death have been greatly exaggerated." Like Twain, assertions about the demise of small towns are not only exaggerated, I contend that they are flat out wrong. In fact, it is the suburbs that may be experiencing a downturn while small towns are being rediscovered for their authentic charm, diversity and uniqueness.

The Deluxe Corporation Small Business Revolution is on to something big with their emphasis on small town main streets which were once the bedrock of America. Society is evolving so quickly that it is often difficult to recognize trends as they are happening. On-line vendors like Zappos, L.L. Bean and, of course, the *United States of Amazon* are exploding. At the same time, we see the large shopping malls falling into decline, with retail giants like Macy's, J.C. Penny and Sears closing stores in dramatic numbers. Their closings will cause a drag on the malls they once anchored and most likely prompt a ripple effect among the smaller retailers that once surrounded them. Time magazine recently reported one out of four malls will close in the next five years, victimized by the relativity easy and highly efficient on-line shopping experience. Over 8000 big name retailers will close this year nationwide. All of this gloom and doom can bode well for smaller communities provided they have effective leadership, a strong community spirit and can articulate a shared vision for who they are and where they are going. The "who they are" part is what's operative here. Main streets will never be the retail hubs they were in their glory days or that malls became. But they can fill the void that mall closings are creating. For a time, malls became the social gathering places, the defacto town squares of a generation, a distinction once held by small town main streets. But main streets can experience a resurgence if they find their niche. For Bristol Borough and similar communities, we believe that niche is dining, the arts and specialty retail, with a strong emphasis upon historic preservation and promoting our natural resources.

I think that people, especially young people, are growing weary of the bland, isolated, homogeneous life of the suburban developments with their contrived names like meadows, woods, estates and court and are finding the cookie-cutter, chain restaurants that dot their suburban landscape less and less appealing. I don't know about you, but I've watched my last gathering of chain restaurant waiters and waitresses at someone's table rolling their eyes as they sing an uninspired rendition of Happy Birthday to an embarrassed customer. I've also seen my last of twenty-page menus offering selections so similar that they wouldn't pass a blind taste test to differentiate one chain from another. People looking for a weekend "night out," want something a little more genuine and varied, both in food and experience. Visiting an area that offers a cluster of original restaurants with an urban feel adds a sense of coolness. Of course, cities offer that, but the city experience comes at a cost of increased travel time, parking frustrations and added expense. The resurgence of small independent restaurants clustered on Main Streets like Bristol's Mill and Radcliffe Streets is a sign of things to come.

I have little doubt that on-line consumerism will continue to flourish, and will account for a growing share of our purchases. But after a hard day at the computer either working, shopping or searching for that perfect romantic match, people will always have a desire to gather and interact with others, and this is where small town main streets can fill an important void. They can become, and in many cases, have already become, the gathering places they once were. And as people visit to dine or enjoy the arts, they are exposed to the specialty shops in proximity to them. Soon there is a widening ripple of economic growth and an increased interest in reasonably priced housing, and the decline in population turns into an increase and that contributes to a growing economy.

We can do this, Small Town America. In Bristol Borough, Pennsylvania, we've already started.

Part I

RAISING THE BAR

Americans love watching sporting events, and marvel at the accomplishments of our most successful athletes on game day. But not nearly enough attention is paid to what those athletes do before, during and after practice to prepare for their contests, to maximize their potential and put themselves in a position to win.

This book is primarily about Historic Bristol Borough's four-month ordeal to win the Deluxe Corporation's national Small-Business Revolution-Main Street contest over 3500 competitors. The win secured a $500,000 infusion of capital and technical assistance to the town's business district, a four-hour nationally released eight-part video series about the town, and all of the positive publicity that surrounded the contest. The victory ranks at the very top of any list of Bristol's finest moments, but *it would be a mistake to view that process in a vacuum.* To be sure, the residents of Bristol Borough and their friends and family near and far responded tremendously to the challenge, but **the achievement would not have been possible without an organizational structure in place to put Bristol in a position to win and exceptional leaders in the past who kept the struggling town on life support for so many years.**

Raising the Bar may have been the civic group that led the charge to win the contest, but it didn't just pop up overnight. It had been developing as a positive force in the town for four years, and any discussion about HOW BRISTOL WON, has to begin with RTB's formation and the philosophy and practices it put in place.

Chapter 1- Stepping Up

In 2017, my son and daughter-in -Law opened a restaurant/bar on Mill Street in Historic Bristol Borough called *itri Wood Fired Pizza Bar.* Watching them go through the eleven- month ordeal of purchasing, gutting and remodeling a building, and spending countless hands-on hours interviewing and hiring staff, building and testing a menu, marketing and doing the thousands of mundane things it takes to open a business, has been exhilarating, instructive and very, very scary. I'm extremely proud of them as well as all of the young, new entrepreneurs like Andrew and Jodi Dittman, Joe Rakowski, Matthew and Michele Howard, Karla Sloan, Tim McGinty and others. I want them to succeed. So, what happens on Mill Street certainly holds my interest.

But years before they started their adventure, and years before Deluxe had even conceptualized the Main Street Revolution here or anywhere else, **I had this borderline compulsion to do something about the struggling street**. Maybe it was the sense of nostalgia I had for my childhood memories of Saturday mornings, when it was at its apex and bustling with vitality. My friends and I bought our colored live chickens at Easter time from McCroy's Five and Ten. We bought our camping equipment from Spector's and then "camped" at Maple Beach with our canteens and backpacks. We visited Len's men's store to buy whatever fad clothing was trending at the time: Neru jackets, hooded windbreakers called Whalers, hip length black leather jackets. It was fun. Maybe it was the nice memory during my courtship with Karen when I'd stop in to Cis Profy's Sports Shop each payday to buy her a blouse or skirt. Cis would show me something and say, this would be perfect for Karen. She was always right. Or maybe my interest in the street was a carryover from my days as Borough Council President in the 1980s, when Councilman Don McCloskey got me hooked by leading the charge to install brick sidewalks, period lighting, and trees there. It was a big deal, and we believed then that the improvements would have a ripple effect on neighboring blocks. Progress ended up being much slower than we had hoped. Maybe my interest stemmed from years of reading and listening to consultants explain that the health of any town begins with a vibrant commercial district, without which nothing else would follow. Maybe I'm just bugged by unrealized potential. Whatever the reason, Mill Street has been my thing, perhaps my obsession.

In 2013, I was especially down about the conditions I saw. There were an alarming number of vacant storefronts which had everyone's attention. But what really bugged me was the appearance of those properties. Some had windows lined with old newspapers that had yellowed with age. Others were covered with wrinkled brown butcher paper. Still others had nothing at all, allowing passersby to see the store just as it was left by the previous tenant, with remnants of previous stock still in place. In those cases, it looked like a Hollywood movie set for a ghost town scene. There were a few properties that were missing pieces of siding, and the weeds, oh those damn weeds!

I was really down. What were these property owners thinking? Where was their pride? Where was their sense of civic responsibility? For that matter, even if they didn't care about the town, which they obviously didn't, where was their sense of acting in their self-interest? Did they believe that a potential renter or buyer would survey the scene and determine this was where they wanted to invest? They were committing a form of slow commercial suicide and they were taking others with them, notably the business owners on the street who were working to manage their own business and had to cope with this environment. It was also draining the spirits of town residents who looked at it every day and just shook their heads.

I'm not sure what the tipping point was for me. Maybe when I began seeing sloppy, hand painted signs on buildings that *were open for business.* I'd say they looked like they were done by third graders, but that would be an insult to third graders. Maybe it was after hearing still another snide remark about Bristol from someone north of Route 1. Whatever it was, one day I just had enough. I remembered the old adage, often repeated by my mother, "If you want something done, do it yourself."

My wife, Karen, and I approached some local photographers like Dave McGlynn and Mary MaGill, who had posted beautiful photos of Bristol scenes on Facebook, like the Grundy clock tower, the wharf, and ethnic monuments. We asked for their permission to have the images blown up and used to cover the windows in vacant stores. They agreed.

Next, we visited the owners of the vacant storefronts for permission to replace the unsightly newspaper with the more desirable blown up photos. We pointed out that not only would this give the street a better appearance, it might increase their chances of finding a tenant or selling the building. The responses were interesting. A couple seemed embarrassed that they hadn't done something similar on their own and offered to help. That was encouraging. As for the rest, their general response was that we could do it as long as it didn't cost them anything. One required a waiver of liability if we became injured on their property. But at least no one said no. We ended up doing eight storefronts.

I have a pretty good idea of what many of you are thinking right now. Why should anyone do the work that property owners should be doing for themselves? Well, the answer is that they weren't doing it and the Borough seemingly lacked the legal ability or the political will to

15

force them (more on that later). So, we did it for the same reason that Jose' Acevedo leads a Keep Bristol Beautiful town-wide cleanup campaign to pick up other people's' litter or Maryjo D'Agostino sweeps the gutters of not only her building but those adjacent to her. We did it for the same reason that Maryann Ennis and Lorraine Hoffman plant flowers in the flower box at Selecto market even though they don't own the store. We did it for the same reason Matt Shaw picks weeds from the traffic island near Old Route 13 at the gateway to our town. You do these things because you're sick of looking at negligence. You do it to improve the appearance of the town. You do it because you want to model good behavior in the hope that the idea will catch on. You do it for the personal satisfaction it brings. You do it because you want to Raise the Bar of expectations we have for ourselves and others. When broken windows or litter or graffiti or unsightly windows become the norm, then you are losing. But when you do something about it, no matter how small, you're winning.

Chapter 2- Mill Street Crossing: Symbolism Matters!

In 1932 Franklin D. Roosevelt was running for president at the height of the Great Depression. To say that millions of Americans were on the verge of despair would be an understatement. After four years of President Hoover's programs, often called "too little, too late," Roosevelt was keenly aware that the American people wanted action. In one of his speeches he had said, "It is common sense to take a method and try it. If it fails, admit it frankly and try another. But above all, try something. Historians would later say it wasn't that the collection of legislation he introduced was totally effective in a tangible sense. It was that his **actions** convinced the American people that someone was **trying** and that boosted their confidence and bolstered their hope.

In 2013, it was no secret that Bristol Borough had been struggling for years. There were successes, but they were sporadic and fragmented. A group of us met to begin the process of developing a plan of economic development and civic involvement. We felt our current Borough Council, led my Council President Ralph DiGuiseppe and Borough Manager Jim Dillon, was doing a very good job. They were progressive and had accomplished a great deal. But it was clear that Bristol Borough's needs were much greater than the Borough government had the time or resources to address. We approached them with an offer to help and made it clear we were there to assist, not compete. We wanted a partnership, not an adversarial relationship. Less secure leaders would have been skeptical of our motives and met the offer with resistance. I've seen it happen numerous times in other towns and other times. Instead, they gave us their blessing, and we were on our way.

After months of work we were nearing the completion of our five-year plan and making arrangements to roll it out to the council and public. We were determined that it wouldn't be just another document to gather dust on a shelf. We wanted it to work. Our primary message was one of citizen involvement. The days of waiting for some outsider, some white knight, to rescue Bristol Borough from its economic stagnation were over. No one was coming. If there were opportunities out there, we'd have to go get them. If there were changes that needed to be made, we'd have to be the catalyst to make them ourselves. This was to be a call to citizen action, a plan of empowerment, where everyone was invited to participate to share their time, talent and treasure to kick start our revival.

We were excited, but knew we faced some early challenges if we wanted to gain the attention and support of the public. The first was the issue of branding. We needed a name, and calling ourselves the Economic Development Committee had all of the excitement of watching paint dry. Someone suggested Revitalization Committee and the idea was dead on arrival. There had been more revitalization committees in the Borough's past than the New England Patriots (those stinkin' cheaters) have Super Bowl rings. We needed something fresh.

Finally, the name Raising the Bar surfaced and we liked it. It had a ring of challenge to it, but also of confidence. We would be elevating the expectations we had for ourselves and others, indeed, for our town. It had an element of movement to it. The idea that the process would never end, that we would always be looking to elevate, to achieve, like that whole, "A person's reach should exceed his grasp," thing. The logo image we selected was designed by Bridget Ennis-Shaw. It depicted a group of silhouetted figures holding a bar above their heads and struggling to raise it higher. We now had a name, a logo and a plan. All we needed now was to engage the public.

We were still in our early stages when one of our committee members said that a group of his neighbors from Radcliffe Street wanted to approach us about an idea they were excited about. We agreed to meet.

Led by Mycle Gorman and Ron McGuckin, the group's pitch was that Borough residents needed to see something tangible happening, a simple but demonstrative project they could get behind that would symbolize the plan we were about to share, something to signify **movement, direction, action**. They proposed to erect a façade- like structure on a borough owned vacant lot at the entrance to Mill Street in our commercial district.   The structure would be called Mill Street Crossing because of its proximity to the former site where the old railroad line, the Delaware Canal and Kings highway had once intersected. **More importantly, we would present it as a symbolic gateway not only to our commercial district, but to the future revival of our town.**

Looking back, what was really striking about the meeting was the dynamic in the room. We didn't own the land or have any money to do the project, but that didn't seem to matter. We were in a room of people who were used to making things happen, and we did. Mycle Gorman owns a design company and he drew the plans for the site. Council President, Ralph DiGuiseppe and Borough Manager, Jim Dillon liked the idea and the council gave us permission to use the land. My wife Karen and I started selling commemorative bricks to help pay for the project and hundreds of residents bought in. Local contractor, Steve Bielecki of R & S donated his crew and equipment and gave us materials at cost. Lou Quattrocchi's Construction Building Materials company donated the use of their boom truck. Rich Valajeo, had just dissolved the corporation that housed the former Mill Street Business Association headquarters and donated a few thousand dollars of the proceeds to the project. The Bristol Borough Veterans Memorial Committee had completed their beautiful memorial project and donated their surplus of almost

$10,000 to Raising the Bar. The project took on a life of its own. It evolved from the original design to meet engineering standards and we dedicated it in time for Historic Bristol day, complete with music from the Bracken Cavaliers Drum and Bugle Corps, and speeches by Congressman Mike Fitzpatrick and other dignitaries. It was a feel-good, broad-based project, and a tangible reminder that Bristol Borough was on its way, that **something was happening**.

Mill Street Crossing taught us three important lessons that can be instructive to others.

1. People like **action.** If you want to make an impact, do something visible. Even if you just move that bolder an inch to start, get it started.
2. **Substance is important, but so is style and symbolism.** Today, four years later, Raising the Bar is one of the most recognizable brands among civic and economic development groups in Bucks County and has already been recognized by the Chamber of Commerce, The Bucks County Planning Commission, The Bucks County Visitors and Tourist commission and, most importantly, **the people of Bristol Borough.**
3. Local governments from here to Timbuktu get criticized for their actions. Especially in towns with limited resources and seemingly unlimited problems. With human nature being what it is, it's easy for elected officials to become guarded and defensive after a while, and suspicious of the goals of others. If you want to get involved and have no agenda other than to help, it's important to convey that message to your elected officials and work to form a partnership. This is obvious but lacking in so many instances. Where there is a strong partnership between government and the private sector, good things can happen.

Chapter 3- Getting People on the Raising the Bar Bus

Good to Great, by Jim Collins was one of the top selling business books in 2001. Its purpose was to illustrate how good companies could become great and to highlight the characteristics that great companies exhibit to sustain themselves. I found that many of Collins' points could be applicable to how a civic organization like Raising the Bar should operate in moving from good to great. I was particularly struck by one metaphor he offered. **He said to be successful an organization has to get the right people on the bus, and then get them in the right seats!**

From our perspective, **Raising the Bar didn't just want to fill a metaphorical bus with volunteers wishing to share their time and talent; we wanted to fill a *caravan.*** From day one we preached that everyone was welcome to join with only one caveat- No boo birds were allowed. We just didn't have time for naysayers. (More on that later). Earlier, I referred to Raising the Bar as a **movement.** That's because we don't have membership as such. There is no induction ceremony, no secret handshake, no annual dues. Yes, we have a nine-member Board of Directors to manage necessary business like raising funds, entering into contracts, paying bills, purchasing insurance, applying for grants, etc. And we have a core group of about twenty-five dedicated people who step up regularly to do the recurring work that needs to be done, but beyond that, everyone is welcome, and we mean it!

But getting people to join an organized effort is easier said than done for several reasons. For starters, it's tough to convince them that they truly are welcome because life's experiences often teach us otherwise. Whether it's memories of a middle school clique we were excluded from or an unwelcoming bridge club at the senior center or maybe just because some people are shy, if an organization wants to recruit effectively, it's important to be mindful of the challenges.

We had a particular challenge to address in Bristol Borough because it is an older, established community with families that can trace their roots there for generations. Whether intentional or not "newcomers" to town can easily feel excluded. I've heard it more than once. "This is a tough town to break into."

I'm reminded of a story from a few years back. We were planning our first Keep Bristol Beautiful town-wide clean up. And we had a group of thirty or so organizers gathered at the Borough community room. I suggested we begin the meeting by giving our names and sharing something about ourselves. The first person said, "My name is Mike and I've been a resident of Bristol for fifteen years. The next person said, "I'm Ann and my husband and I have lived here all of our lives." I knew there were some new faces in the room and didn't like where this was going. Before the next person could speak, I said, "Look, I'm proud of my Bristol heritage too, but **when it comes to volunteers, Raising the Bar doesn't care if you've been in town for fifteen years or fifteen minutes. If you want to become part of something positive, we've got a place for you**. So, let's try again without the genealogy." We laughed about it and then went on. Those first two speakers were wonderful people who would never want to exclude anyone. But it was important to note that their innocent profession of their town roots might make someone new feel less than welcome. The clean-up program ended up attracting over three hundred volunteers, broken into small groups with each talking responsibility for a street or neighborhood. It was well planned and we ended up gathering seven truckloads of litter. (More later on the idea of organizing neighborhoods to Raise the Bar).

Feeling unwelcome is not the only reason why some are reluctant to volunteer. Some may fear getting "stuck" in a task they won't enjoy or a project that will consume too much of their time. They may also feel that they do not have the skills we're looking for. Again, an effective organization is cognizant of these very real concerns and addresses them. At Raising the Bar, in addition to doing the best we can to convey that all are welcome, we have a simple motto that we've found effective. "Do only what you enjoy doing, for only the amount of time you are willing to give." With that arrangement clearly understood up front, people are more likely to step up. We also have success when we put a time limit to a project. For example, asking who can help hang flower baskets on the light poles on Main Street (Mill Street in our case) is more likely to be successful if we add "for one hour only."

As Collins said in his book, after we get the people on the "bus," it's important to get them in the right seats. For us, this means matching people's special skills or interests with projects that need to be done. The person willing to help with webpage design may not like to pick weeds. The person who enjoys physical work like hanging flower baskets on Mill Street may not feel suited to write a grant proposal that we'd like to submit. Obviously, people do what they enjoy and shy away from things they don't. Probably one of the most satisfying aspects of the Raising the Bar experience has been watching people step forward to lend their special skills or interests to Raising the Bar projects.

The result has been a strong core of people who carry the ball on a regular basis, a larger number nearing three hundred who step up for major projects like town wide cleanups, and people literally in the thousands who responded to the call for the Small Business Revolution.

So, the take-away from the Bus analogy is:

1. Welcome everyone (except the boo birds) to participate and mean it. They won't believe you at first, but keep driving home that Raising the Bar is not a clique, it's a movement. When we worked to bring the Clydesdales to town, we had to

supply Anheuser-Bush and Gretz Beer Company with an honor guard of twelve people to walk alongside of the horses and carriage to keep the crowd back. We could have easily picked twelve "insiders." Instead, we selected the escorts by lottery. People loved the idea, and it sent a terrific message about inclusion.

2. Avoid the square peg in the round hole syndrome. Ask people to do only what they enjoy and they'll keep coming back.

3. Don't waste people's time. Having meetings for the sake of meetings is counter- productive. If you're going to have a meeting, make it meaningful or don't have it. More than one volunteer has said they are busy but here for us when we need them. They've done great work for us as grant writers, graphic designers, event planners. They step up only when we need them, and that works for us.

Chapter 4- Millennials and Perennials

In January of 1961, forty-three-year-old John F. Kennedy was sworn in as the youngest elected president in American History. He said many memorable things in his brilliantly crafted inaugural address. One line that stood out for me was this: "Let the word go forth from this time and place ... that the torch has been passed to a new generation of Americans." Indeed, it had. President Eisenhower, who had been a type of grandfather image for the country, was leaving office at the age of seventy-one. The relatively youthful Kennedy had appointed the youngest cabinet to date in American History to help him lead.

So where am I going with this? Not where you might think. In the time-honored debate about whether youthful vigor vs. aged experience is preferable as a leadership trait, I come down strongly on both sides. Much has been written about *Millennials,* and they'll be addressed here, but I'd like to coin a new term for people at the opposite end of the age spectrum- *Perennials.* And I use the term affectionately, perhaps because I'm one of them.

Consider this. The core team of twenty-five workers who organized and led the daily charge to win the Small Business Revolution for Bristol Borough and do the brunt of the work for Raising the Bar, have an average age well beyond eligibility for AARP membership. To a person, they were energized, organized, dependable and capable. I'd gladly partner with them to take on any project and be confident of the outcome. An organization or community that ignores or underutilizes perennials is making a serious mistake. The stereotype of the senior citizen (Oh, how I hate that term) as someone who catches the 4:00 PM early bird special at Cracker Barrell before returning home to watch NCIS reruns is grossly inaccurate. So is sixty is the new fifty outlook. In many cases it's more like sixty is the new forty-five.

There are some valuable assets that the perennials have that their younger counterparts do not. First, of course, is experience. Pick your cliché: They've been around the block a few times. This is not their first rodeo…yada, yada, yada. But it's true, and they've picked up some valuable knowledge and skills along the way. It would be foolish for an organization to waste them. Perhaps their greatest asset is the precious commodity of time. Their kids are grown. They are retired. They don't sleep as much as their youthful counterparts. More hours in the day means more productivity. They also have a need to find renewed meaning in their lives, something to latch on to so as to fill the void once filled with their employment. They are an inexpensive resource because they are dependable volunteers. They enjoy better healthcare than their parents did and are healthier and live longer as a result.

There is one more asset of the perennials I'm compelled to add, a bit tongue in check. Those people of the 1930s, 40s and 50s who survived the Great Depression, stormed the beaches at Normandy to save the world from tyranny and returned home to build a thriving middle-class economy, clearly were, beyond a doubt, as Tom Brokaw called them, The Greatest Generation, and it's sad that most of them are gone. But today's perennials, the baby boomers who came of age in the 1960s, are clearly the coolest generation. (It's my book and I can say that.) They revolutionized popular culture with their music, art and literature, fought for civil rights and gender equality, embraced the environment, rejected hypocrisy, threw away their neckties, loosened things up and made blue jeans their generational uniform. They often think and act younger than their parents did.

Having said all that, we can't avoid the obvious. Any organization needs a healthy influx of younger people to step up, to play leadership roles. It won't be easy. Many analysts have said Millennials are too self-absorbed to make a difference. I disagree. They are a valuable asset, tech savvy, and tuned in to the urban chic movement that exists in the cities and in small towns like Bristol Borough that are rediscovering themselves.

Bristol Borough and Raising the Bar will need an influx of young people to continue the work we have started and we're committed to getting younger people involved in charting the course. Justin Saxton, an employee of Construction Building Materials in town, is one of our RTB board members. Recently honored as an emerging young leader by the Lower Bucks County Chamber of Commerce, he was a driving force in our Smell Business Revolution contest and is a valuable resource in maintaining our social media presence.

Luke Wade is our newest board member. Appointed this year, he is nineteen years old and will be starting his undergraduate work at Drexel University this fall. Luke is bright, mature beyond his years, passionate about his town, knowledgeable about social media, and a good sounding board about what younger people are thinking. There is also a growing number of young entrepreneurs emerging like Greg and Dana Pezza of *itri wood Fired Pizza and Bar*, Paulette Kasmer of Polka Dot Parlor, Matthew Howard at Healthy Plate Meal Preps, Tim McGinty at Mill Street Cantina, and Joe Rakowski at Nobel Earth and many more, who will be contributing to the vibe of the "new" Mill Street.

As we work to attract younger people to Bristol Borough, either as visitors or first-time home buyers, it's important for the town leaders to recognize that they are looking for cool, quality of life amenities like dog parks, jogging paths, kayak and jet ski access to the river, organic food outlets, bicycle racks, murals, the arts, dining and entertainment. We're well on our way with some of these and need to step up our efforts in others.

Millennials and *Perennials and everyone in between, working side by side. We need them all.*

Chapter 5- CAUTION: Boo Birds Can Be Hazardous to Your Success.

Monsignor Joseph Ferrara is a wonderful priest originally from Saint Ann parish in Bristol Borough. He joined the navy and saw the world as a Chaplin. He's getting up there in years now, but he occasionally returns to say Mass in his home town, always to a full house. He often begins with a welcoming joke. I'm not sure where he gets them, but they're always good. Then he says, "Sit down and relax. I'm certain that something in this Mass today will touch you in a special way." Something always does.

Anyway, that's the way it is with me and books. If I can grab one worthwhile thing that sticks with me to carry forward, then it was worth reading. I once read a best-seller by Dr. Eric Berne titled, *Games People Play*. Later Thomas Harris built upon Berne's work with the popular *I'm Ok; You're Ok*, which was a guide to transactional analysis. (Damn, I'm already sorry I used that term and promise not to again. Hope you're still reading). For our purposes of putting together a winning, civic minded team, the premise is simple. By learning to recognize "games" people engage in with their conversations, tweets or Facebook posts, we can become more effective in identifying and recruiting the type of people who "do" and avoiding those who just "boo."

In *I'm Ok, You're Ok*, Harris describes a game he calls, "Ain't it Awful." People play it all the time, and we can get sucked into it unless we learn to recognize it and nip it in the bud. If we're not careful, it can dampen our spirit and sap the enthusiasm of ourselves or the group we work with.

You may remember the Debbie Downer character from the *Saturday Night Live* TV show. Of course, she took it to an extreme, but in her skits, every time someone shared something positive or upbeat, she followed it with a negative and the air was sucked out of the room.

Here's one of my favorites.

A group is at a restaurant excited about ordering a great dinner. One person says, "I think I'm going to have the steak!" Others enthusiastically agree. Then Debbie Downer says, "I've stopped eating steak ever since I've learned about Mad Cow disease. It enters your body and eventually attacks your brain."

Wow. Debbie obviously broke the positive mood a little. But now the group is at a crucial point in their discourse, because if another person buys in and starts talking about the dangerously high level of mercury in fish, then we're off to an "Ain't it awful" free for all, with one bleak "top this" comment after another, and there goes that wonderful evening.

Of course, this is a comedic example in a social setting. No real harm is done other than a ruined evening. You'll get over it. But in the context of a civic group that is engaging in problem solving or goal setting or planning to launch an initiative, the Debbie Downers and "Ain't it awful" players of the world can obviously be destructive to your success and dampen the morale of your team.

Whether we're talking about Bristol Borough or any other small town, surmounting our challenges is hard enough without someone throwing a wet blanket over what would otherwise be a spark of enthusiasm for an idea by stating why you cannot, should not, or better not do something. Some are experts at it. They revel in it. They excel at being negative.

Let me be clear, meaningful dialogue about the pros and cons of a project or strategy are necessary and can ultimately make an idea stronger. But what we're talking about here is the difference between people who offer a sincere examination of an issue with a positive goal in mind and those who just love to put out the fire of enthusiasm.

It is so much easier to say something can't be done than it is to roll up your sleeves and try to make it happen. Be keenly aware of the difference and when you see a downer, run away as fast as you can before you get infected with the negative flu because it can be highly contagious.

Chapter 6- When You See a Good Idea, Steal It!

A college professor once told me that the best way to be successful is to study the success of others. When we think we know everything we miss out on learning from those who know more. When we are humble enough to emulate proven practices, then we're on the right track. "Doing so isn't a sign of weakness," he said. "It's a sign of strength." It was good advice, and a couple of examples come to mind.

Field Marshall Erwin Rommel was a brilliant World War II tank commander in the German Wehrmacht, fighting in Northern Africa where his many successes earned him the nickname, The Desert Fox. Prior to World War II, he had written a book about battle tactics which had won him his command. Legendary American General, George S. Patton was tasked with stopping German advances and driving their forces out of Africa. After one decisive American victory, Patton reportedly exclaimed, "Rommel, you magnificent bastard, I read your book!" Clearly Patton understood how to borrow from the successes of others.

Here's another example closer to home. I was the offensive coordinator for a high school football team in the 1970s, and we had a decent squad. But on one occasion we traveled to Springfield High School in Montgomery County for a non-league game, and what happened next was astonishing. Springfield led 48-0 at halftime!

Mercifully, Springfield's coach, Al Black, substituted heavily in the second half and the final score was 48-20. Nevertheless, it was clear that we were outcoached. I mean, really outcoached.

In the off-season, our staff attended a coaching clinic in Atlantic City and we ran into Al Black. He invited us to a side conference for coaches who ran his system, the one that had humbled us the previous season. We went. If Black had something to say, then, like George S. Patton, I was going to soak up all that I could. Black saw me taking extensive notes and said, "I just wrote a book on this stuff, why don't you just buy it?"

I did, and I read it from cover to cover - twice. We implemented his system the following year, and (I know this will sound like a tall tale, but it's true), we won the league championship five out of the next six years. It's been almost forty years since I coached, but Al Black's book, *Modern Belly-T Football*, still occupies a place of prominence on my book shelf as a reminder of the importance of seeking out people who know more than you do and soaking up all you can from them.

But this isn't a book about football or tank tactics; it's a book about small town planning, and there is a parallel story that is relevant here.

Amy McIlvaine has been a friend and exemplary citizen of Bristol for as long as I can remember. She's bright, well-educated and has a significant professional network. It was a no brainer that I'd ask her to be part of the economic development planning committee we were putting together for the town.

During our planning process, we knew that no small town could ever again compete commercially with the malls, big box stores and the growing internet retail presence. We had to find our niche, our special place in the commercial world, and we settled upon four pillars: dining, the arts, historic preservation and specialty retail. What followed was a discussion of other small towns or neighborhoods like Media, Pennsylvania and the Manayunk section of Philadelphia that had reinvented themselves following that formula.

At that point Amy asked if we were familiar with the Collingswood, New Jersey success story. Collingswood shared many characteristics with Bristol. It was a former middle-class factory town with strong roots and a diverse population. As the national economy changed, Collingswood, like small towns across America, had fallen on hard times until it reinvented itself with great success using the formula we planned to implement. Amy said the driving force behind the transformation was Mayor James Maley. And, no surprise, Amy had some sort of Kevin Bacon like, friend- of-a -friend connection to him. She suggested it might be a good idea to invite him to meet with us.

We traveled to Collingswood, and the town proved to be a model of what we hoped Bristol could achieve, with a thriving, vibrant commercial district that preserved the charm and character of the old community. We followed the visit with an invitation to the mayor to visit Bristol Borough to speak at a town meeting we would sponsor at the Bristol Riverside Theater.

Mayor Maley proved to be as gracious as he was knowledgeable. He agreed to the visit and declined our offer of a speaker's fee. That was a very good sign, not because we saved a few dollars, but because it spoke volumes about his passion and dedication to his work. I was also impressed to learn that he intentionally arrived in town an hour early so that he could quietly tour our Mill Street commercial district and riverfront to assess our assets and challenges.

Raising the Bar had promoted the meeting heavily and charged $10 for admission. We felt that not charging would diminish the way people would view the night. We wanted people to know that this was important, and ascribing a modest fee to a ticket would help drive that message home. We sold 320 tickets and filled the space.

At the town hall, Maley reaffirmed much of what we were thinking, but it was good for our citizens to hear it from an outside source with a proven track record. It was also encouraging to learn that he felt in some ways Bristol Borough was better positioned to be successful because of our easy access to the riverfront. He stressed how vital it was to form a partnership with government officials at all levels, especially local councilpersons, *and to convince them that, as private volunteers, we were there to help not compete.*

During our visit, we had noticed that Collingswood had banners surrounding their theater designating the area as their theater district. Someone asked how to go about establishing a district for Bristol Borough. Maley smiled and said, "Do what we did. Just put up the signs. This is your town. You can do what you want." He was right. This was another lesson in symbolism and branding. Soon Raising the Bar partnered with Landmark Towns and the Grundy Foundation to put up tasteful signs designating the area from the monuments along the riverfront, to the Bristol Riverside Theater along Radcliffe Street to the Grundy Museum and Library as the **Bristol Borough Cultural Corridor.**

Finally, he talked about dealing with dissenters, and I found this to be the best advice. He said we will always have those who will criticize our goals and practices. He advised that it was best to approach them directly, and exchange as much information as possible. Often people disagree because they don't understand. But once that dialogue is over, if some were still opposed to the broad plan, and some certainly would be, we should follow our convictions and move full speed ahead. Too many movements fall victim to trying to please everyone and sacrifice their momentum in the process.

Looking back, Maley's visit was a defining moment for Bristol Borough and Raising the Bar. It reaffirmed our goals. It demonstrated, by virtue of our sold-out audience, that there was a strong grass roots desire to move forward. Finally, it raised the spirits of those in attendance who would form the core group of those who would play an active role in our future progress.

1. Search for the best practices of those who are successful and incorporate whatever fits.
2. Mycle Gorman one of our board members and a dynamo of energy and vision likes to say, "Get on board or get out of the way," sometimes in less artful terminology. But, after all, we have work to do…

Chapter 7- Opening the Centre for the Arts

It was opening night for our Celebration of Labor exhibit at the Center for the Arts. As usual, the space was packed and Raising the Bar was basking in the glow of our gallery's success. Many had said that an art gallery could never work in the lower end of the county, especially Bristol Borough. The arts were celebrated in the more affluent and picturesque areas of Central Bucks County in places like Newtown, New Hope and Doylestown, all of which were indeed thriving. But we saw dining, the arts, and specialty retail as the keys to a resurgence to Bristol Borough's downtown district and the ripple effect they would have on the broader community.

The story of how Raising the Bar opened a gallery is instructive about how vision, guts and hard work can make things happen. A year earlier we were gathered at Carl White, Jr.'s house at one of our floating meetings that always featured a healthy mixture of food, drink and business. That night, Ron McGuckin, said that since Raising the Bar existed to promote tourism and economic development, we needed to ensure that visitors had something to do when they visit besides eat. Heads nodded. Then he dropped the bombshell, "We should put our money where our mouths are and open a Center for the Arts."

This was another defining moment for our group. Of the fifteen people in the room, no one debunked the idea or dwelled on the number of challenges we would face. Instead, what followed was a spirited and visionary brainstorming session about exhibits, art and music lessons, possible locations on Mill Street and funding sources. Whether it was blind optimism or confidence buoyed by the wine served that night, by the end of the meeting it was clear- WE WERE GOING TO OPEN AN ART CENTER. We weren't sure how or exactly where yet, but we were committed to do it.

A week later we met for breakfast at the Golden Eagle Dinner to talk further. Toast and coffee are far more conducive to sober business planning than wine and cheese. An opportunity had presented itself. A local bank had foreclosed on a once popular shoe store. It was a large building suitable to our needs and the price had been steadily dropping. We had a serious discussion about estimated costs for a mortgage, renovations, taxes, utilities and insurance as well as potential revenue from gallery and studio fees. The numbers seemed to work. But...there is always a but... I remember tuning to Joanna Schneyder, an RTB board member and retired banker to ask about the mortgage process. Joanna is a warm, talented and generous person. But you know how bankers are when they put their banker's hat on, always working from their head instead of their heart. I guess it has something to do with sound business practice. Anyway, she smiled politely and said, "Raising the Bar has no recurring income, and no bank will give you a mortgage."

I suddenly had a cartoon image of a hot air balloon with Centre for the Arts printed on the side losing altitude because the flame had gone out on the burner and the passengers were frantically looking for a match to relight it. To make matters worse, the waitress chose just then to arrive with the check. That actually turned out to be a blessing because it gave Ron Walker a minute or so to gather his thoughts before dropping the next bombshell. "I'll finance the building," he said flatly after the waitress left. That took a minute to register. Before we could respond, he added, "the building and a reasonable amount for renovations. You'll pay the going interest rate. It should be no problem."

I should add here that PR is my gig, give me an event to promote and I'll fill the room, but my business experience consists of a paper route I had in eighth and ninth grade. In moments like these I defer to the adults in the room. In this case, Ron McGuckin, who is also the RTB attorney, put on his best pondering face, rubbed his chin and said that would work just fine. Joanna agreed, and we were on our way again.

Right after we acquired the building, we were eager to get started with renovations and still a little anxious about how things would go. I posted a message on our Raising the Bar Facebook page asking for volunteers to help tear up 3000+ square feet of old carpeting. That Saturday thirty-two people showed up and we were finished in two hours! That was an immensely satisfying and instructive experience for me. If there was any doubt about whether we'd be successful, it was dispelled by the spirit and enthusiasm of the volunteers that day.

We were determined to make the building a showplace, so we gutted it and Mycle Gorman designed and supervised the renovation. We soon learned that Mycle goes about his business blissfully unencumbered by budget constraints. They tend to stifle his creativity. But damn, he does beautiful work, as does Rich Schneyder, a true craftsman, who did the construction.

When the building was completed we hosted an open house for artists which drew a big crowd (I think I mentioned something earlier about filling a room) and by the end of the night I held deposits on EVERY FOOT OF WALL SPACE IN THE GALLERY. Since then the gallery has been named "Best in Bucks," in the prestigious Bucks County Courier Times contest, Best Gallery in the *Bucks Happening* on-line magazine contest, and *Member of the Year* by the Arts and Cultural Council of Bucks County. Not too shabby.

Two years later, the bills are being paid, the gallery is thriving, and is staffed by volunteers. Our events room has become a popular spot for baby showers, anniversary and birthday celebrations, rehearsal dinners, exhibits and musical performances. But equally important is the fact that the project gave people a chance to step up, to have ownership and a sense of belonging to something positive.

Like Mill Street Crossing, the Centre for the Arts became a visual symbol that positive things were on the horizon for Bristol Borough.

Today the gallery is open thirty-three hours per week and is staffed entirely by volunteers.

So, was the opening of the Centre for the Arts a big deal? You bet it was.

1. *It reaffirmed for Raising the Bar that there were indeed people out there who wanted to be involved and would be if empowered.*
2. *It gave our residents another tangible symbol that something new was happening in our commercial district.*
3. *It gave impetus to the growing art scene in Bristol Borough.*

Chapter 8- Media Relations

If a tree falls in the woods and no one is around to hear it, does it still make a noise? This thought teaser has been a popular discussion prompt in philosophy classrooms for centuries. A similar question in marketing classrooms might be, if a major event occurs and the media doesn't cover it, did it really happen? Marketers and promoters yearn for wide-spread exposure of whatever they're "selling." But with unlimited requests for coverage and limited staff and resources to address them all, media outlets constantly make judgments about what to include and what to omit. At the turn of the 20th Century, Adolph S. Ochs, the owner of *The New York Times,* created the famous slogan, "All the News That's Fit to Print." It is still on the NYT masthead one-hundred years later. In all media circles editors decide what is "fit" to print by deciding which story to cover, whether to place it on the front page or bury it in section C, and how much space it will receive. The question is: Do we as promoters sit back and "hope" we get coverage of our events or do we do all we can to understand the needs and challenges of the media outlets so we can more effectively get their attention and facilitate their efforts.

As we set out to "sell" the idea that something new and different was happening in Bristol Borough, we knew the importance of cultivating good media relations. Looking forward, RTB clearly did a great job with media relations during the 2017 SBR contest. But those relationships didn't happen overnight. It was a long process of building trust and knowing the special needs and requirements of the various outlets. It was a process that began in 2014 and was worth the effort.

Let me say at the outset that Bristol Borough would not have won the 2017 Small Business Revolution without the extensive exposure and skillful reporting by the *Bucks County Courier-Times/Intelligencer.* We also received wonderful coverage from the on-line news publication, *LevittownNow*; the *Bucks County Advance*; the *Bristol Times*, and WBCB radio. All played a dramatic role, and all have our gratitude. But as the publication with the largest circulation, the Courier-Times/Intelligencer led the way.

They covered the event because it was news, but I'd like to think that we played an important role in ensuring the coverage by providing the things that journalists need to do their jobs. We pitched the stories to the editors. We wrote informative press releases in the format expected. We arranged for key players to be available for quotes. We made follow-up phone calls to reporters and editors. We were mindful of keeping the story alive by providing periodic updates. We provided positive feedback when stories did appear. We posted links to on-line versions of their articles on Facebook and we took advantage of invitations to write guest editorials.

It was a feel-good story and the media ran with it.

I get a little frustrated at times with friends who like to slam the media for what they feel is a lack of positive coverage. I often hear after a nice event, "Why wasn't the paper here for this?" Here's a little free advice. First, have realistic expectations. Think of it in baseball terms. If you get a hit three out of ten times at the plate, you're having a great year. If you're looking for a home run story, the 2016 World Champion Chicago Cubs hit one every thirty-two at bats. Don't expect more success than that. News organizations are understaffed. Think of that as you're trying to get their attention. Every town and organization is competing for positive coverage. You won't always get it. In your press releases and phone calls, paint a picture of why your story is special. Also, keep in mind that most major news outlets don't cover fluff like ribbon cuttings and check presentations. If you expect them to, you'll be disappointed. Think of a way to package your event as news, not fluff, and you'll improve your success. Everyone has an Easter Egg Hunt. Everyone has a Little League

Opening. Everyone has new business openings. Provide the media with an added twist that makes yours special and maybe…

A word about the film/broadcast media. Giving local TV network affiliates a story a week or two in advance won't mean much. Here's how most of the Philadelphia news stations operate. They meet about mid-morning each day to review the stories they are aware of and decide where to dispatch their film crews for that afternoon and evening. But there are no guarantees because if a watermain breaks and floods the Turnpike or a tractor trailer flips, the program director may redirect a crew to the developing story.

Knowing this process, here's how we approached the TV stations in Philadelphia during the contest. I would send them an email with relevant information including my contact number and address the day before the scheduled event. I would follow it with the same e-mail the morning of the event. Then I would call thirty-minutes later to ask if they received it. In most cases that draws their attention to it and their response is usually something like, "I have it right here and we'll be discussing it this morning." The stations operate at warp speed. If you can get them to look at a story pitch and discuss it, you've done well.

For those of you who might think this approach is overkill, close your eyes and visualize the loaded e-mail inbox of a busy TV program director. Imagine him or her skimming most proposals rather than giving them close review. I prefer to be proactive in increasing the likelihood that our story will be noticed and considered. I guess it works because we had film crews at seven of our events during the contest and aftermath. I'd say that was pretty good.

I said earlier that the Raising the Bar brand had become one of the most recognized civic groups in Bucks County. That wouldn't be the case were it not for the media coverage we worked at. We wanted to make sure that if a tree fell in the woods people would hear about it.

1. To increase the likelihood of news coverage, know what the media outlets expect and provide it.
2. If at first you don't succeed... Again, have realistic expectations of success and keep trying

Chapter 9- Social Media

Let me state the obvious; social media, especially Facebook, Twitter, Instagram and YouTube, is an essential, powerful, cost-effective marketing tool. Used properly, it can get a message out to a large, targeted audience in real time. Everyone pretty much knows that, right? They should by now because according to the Pew Research Center, the number of adults who regularly use social media has increased ten-fold over the past decade, and most of that growth has taken place over the past four years. In spite of that surge, a surprising number of businesses and civic groups have yet to develop a social media presence.

Fortunately, Raising the Bar's ascendance has closely coincided with the recent social media explosion. In fact, having paid due homage to the role the print and broadcast media played in our Small Business Revolution victory, it's fair to add that social media played an equal role in the growth of the Raising the Bar communication network, which later paved the way to the SBR win.

We know that people love to use Facebook to post family events like anniversaries, graduations, birthdays, children and grandchildren, vacations, their favorite dish at their favorite restaurant and more. It's a nice way for people to remain connected. But for our purposes, we wanted it to be a vehicle for our target audience of potential volunteers and consumers to know what Raising the Bar was doing.

We launched a Facebook group titled, Bristol Borough: Raising the Bar, to promote business development, special events, dining, the arts, retail, recreation and historic preservation in the Borough. Because it's mission is to promote, we accept only POSITIVE posts. Anyone who accepts this premise is invited to join the group and post and react as they wish. We started with our core group of twenty-five like-minded people and asked them to recommend others, who in turn recommended others. Since its inception, the group has grown to over 4000 members. Success breeds success, and each time we accomplish a well-publicized goal, we experience a surge in new member requests.

By encouraging followers to post about THEIR programs or establishments, we increase the likelihood that they will expand our base. As I wrote earlier, the print media does very little to publicize what they call fluff. We revel in it. We also use it for calls to action. When we needed volunteers to help with some demo work on the new art center, we got them from our RTB Facebook presence, the same is true for the town-wide cleanup, hanging flower baskets in our commercial district, and more. We provide an avenue for the theater to advertise plays, the Lions to advertise their summer concert series, the Business association and restaurant association to advertise their latest initiatives. We encourage business establishments and civic organizations to post links to their own Facebook pages and websites.

It's free, it's informative, and people love it.

I'm taking the time to review what is obvious to so many in order to reach out to the thirty-five percent of adults and twenty percent of businesses that still do not use social media. Occasionally I'll encounter people who tell me that they missed a particular event and wished they had known about it. When I tell them we promoted it extensively on Facebook, they reply that they're not on Facebook because they don't want everyone knowing their business. I get that. I'm not especially interested in seeing a photo of someone's martini glass or lobster tail dinner. I tell them they can join as an observer. They can create a skeletal profile, never make a friend request or post a status or react to what they see. They can join the Facebook group, observe everything and still maintain their privacy. That invitation goes to everyone reading this.

A few more thoughts about our social media presence.

1. While we restrict posts to only those that promote Bristol Borough happenings, we welcome non-residents to join the group to keep informed. We want them to visit our theater, restaurants and shops and to generally keep abreast of what is going on.
2. We use posts to fund-raise. When we wanted to sell engraved bricks to finance our Mill Street Crossing project, we publicized the idea on Facebook and raised thousands. When we wanted to hang American flags on our Mill Street light poles, the donations came via Facebook posts.
3. We have spotlighted restaurants and businesses on a rotating basis to create a mini "flash mob" effect. A simple statement like, "let's all go to Café Bombay for diner Thursday," has filled the restaurant.
4. NO BOO BIRDS ALLOWED!

I've taught American History and Government for longer than I care to remember, aad I'm madly, hopelessly in love with James Madison, the father of our constitution and author of the Bill of Rights. I consider the first amendment protections the most precious of those rights because it allows us to speak out against tyranny. It also gives freedom to our artists and writers to express themselves as they see fit. American is great because we have a marketplace of ideas that shape our own. Voltaire is widely credited with the famous quote, "*I disapprove of what you say, but I will defend to the death your right to say it.*" I agree, although it's a bit dramatic for a discussion about Facebook.

Having said that, I think I made it pretty clear about our views on what we call Boo Birds. They can suck the enthusiasm out of a group or launch a game of "Ain't it awful" in three seconds flat. This is especially true on Facebook. One negative post can change the dynamic of an event or organization we're promoting. We avoid that by monitoring the site and promptly deleting anything that contradicts our purpose.

I once had someone tell me that he had a constitutional right to post negative things on our site. Once I stopped laughing, I explained that was pure nonsense. He was of course, half right. He has a constitutional right to post his views on HIS site, but not ours.

Consider a crowd entering a sports stadium. We all have a constitutional right to protections against unreasonable searches and seizures. We waive that right when we choose to enter under stadium their rules to search our bags.

This is America. If you want to exercise your right to free speech, then by all means, do so. But ours is a site created by private citizens designed to promote and share positive developments. If you need to be negative, do it on your own site.

Chapter 10- Keeping Up with Success

The good thing about success is that it breeds success, but with it comes added challenges. There is a world of opportunities out there for small towns and the more energized our citizens become the more they see Bristol Borough in a position to capitalize on them. As the organization that led the charge for the SBR win as well as other successes, people naturally gravitate to Raising the Bar with their ideas. We love it. It's visionary, and it beats the heck out of having a lethargic populous.

But positive as it is, the steady flood of ideas about what we "should do," also presents several challenges. Remember that EVERYTHING we do is done by volunteers. RTB is fortunate to have four highly capable grant writers in Laura Wallick, Ron McGuckin, Jim Sell and Robin Butrey. Ann Kohn, Donna McCloskey and Dana Barber also do great work for the BRT, the Grundy Museum and Library respectively, but our initiatives will be asked to give only the amount of time you are comfortable giving.

Another challenge is simply having the workforce required to implement all of the good ideas that surface, and it's complicated. Having too many balls in the air at once reduces effectiveness. We don't want to overextend, but saying we can't do something that could be a home run dampens enthusiasm. We need to prioritize our initiatives and recruit additional capable volunteers to carry the ball with the overload.

Chapter 11- Networking

The history of racial repression in the south included intimidation and violence directed at any attempt by African-Americans to exercise their First Amendment right to peacefully assemble. Group meetings were viewed with suspicion and organizers were terrorized. The one exception to this was Sunday worship at Black churches where attendees were left alone. Ministers often used the relative safety of the pulpit to combine their spiritual message with social commentary.

As Black leaders sought to organize in the late 1950s and 1960s, they recognized that their churches could provide an effective opportunity to network throughout the south. Discrete mid-week phone calls to a collection of ministers could result in a message being transmitted to thousands of African-Americans by Sunday morning. Martin Luther King, Jr. brought this concept to the highest level as the first president of the newly formed Southern Christian Leadership Conference. That organization, a collection of ministers from throughout the south, was widely credited with promoting the August, 1963 March on Washington, where a quarter-of-a-million people watched King deliver his "I Have A Dream" speech. The network was so effective that it created a backlash of Klan violence. A month after King's speech, a Black church in Birmingham, Alabama was bombed and several Black churches across Mississippi were later burned. In spite of the violence, the Civil Rights Movement continued to grow and resulted in the victorious passage of the Civil Rights Act of 1964 and the Voting Rights act of 1965.

An obvious but highly important lesson can be taken from this dramatic episode in history. To accomplish a broad- based goal, it is advisable to develop an effective network of like-minded participants through which to organize and communicate. The networking lesson is just as applicable to small towns striving to move forward as it is to a national movement.

In the fall of 2015, a full year before any of us had ever heard of the Small Business Revolution contest, Raising the Bar had just led a well-attended town wide cleanup and we were thrilled with the results. But in spite of our success, I thought we could do better. Bristol Borough is blessed with numerous civic and social service organizations that do great work in town. I considered how effective it would be if we could develop an apparatus through which all of the groups could easily communicate and respond to a future call for action.

Soon after, Raising the Bar hosted a leadership breakfast and invited the president of every organization in town: The Lions, the Rotary, the business association, ethnic groups, cultural groups, churches, the historic society, arts groups, the Borough Council, the garden club, the hospital, the library, the museum and more. In all, more than sixty town leaders came. We had promised to limit the meeting to one hour so attendees could get to their daily responsibilities. The group was so large that we barely got past our introductions and collection of contact information before our time was up, but we'd taken an important step toward mobilizing for whatever the future held.

It didn't require a brain surgeon to come up with the idea, but it had not been done before. We now had a valuable organizational tool. Little did we know then, that a year later it would be put to good use in winning the SBR contest.

Part II

Winning the Small Business Revolution

Walter Payton was one of the greatest NFL running backs who ever lived. Watching his speed, power and versatility on game day was majestic. But what I remember most about him came from an article I read in a sports magazine. The article focused on the incredible conditioning regimen he put himself through in order to make it look easy on the field. It was a great reminder of how we can applaud achievement in all walks of life without fully appreciating the preparation required to achieve it.

Winning the Small Business Revolution was certainly a majestic moment for Historic Bristol Borough, but the achievement rises to a new level if we fully appreciate the work done by so many over an extended period of time that made it possible.

Part II traces the intensive series of events that spanned a ten-month period from the time Bristol entered the contest until the final film episode of the Season 2 series ended. It is offered here primarily to thank and recognize those who did so much, and to serve as a model for those who follow.

*I decided to begin this section of the book at the end of the story, with the joyous February 22nd announcement of Bristol's win and then go back to the very beginning of the contest to report on what we did step by step **together.***

No doubt I've omitted a person or group that played a significant role in the contest. I apologize in advance. It was, and has been, a crazy time. I also want to remind the reader that four other towns were working just as hard to win as we were. I hope their effort left them all more unified, organized and ready to move forward with other initiatives for their towns. See Appendix II for more on this.

Chapter 12- The February 22nd Announcement

It was February 22, 2017, the day Deluxe corporation was scheduled to announce which of the five small town finalists spread across the country, would be declared the winner of their Small Business Revolution Main Street contest. It was a national competition and the stakes were high, a $500,000 infusion of capital improvements, technical assistance, marketing assistance, and an eight-part video series exclusively focused on the winning town. But the prizes didn't matter to me on that day. I just wanted to win for the sake of winning. So many people with no direct stake in business and with nothing tangible to gain had fully immersed themselves in the contest for no other reason than town pride. They deserved a win. They needed a win. Historic Bristol Borough, which had once been called a gritty little town, and which wasn't always held in the highest esteem by the rest of the more affluent Buck County, needed something to lift the spirit of its people and polish its image. We needed a confidence builder, something that would keep residents believing that our long history of economic boom, bust and supposed resurgence would indeed result in a resurgence.

Raising the Bar had reserved the Bristol Riverside Theater so that three hundred residents could watch the live-streamed announcement together. The announcement by Deluxe Corporation's chief branding officer, Amanda Brinkman, was scheduled for 2:00 PM, and we were told to ensure that our planned pre- announcement program at the theater would be completed by 1:50.

People began arriving at noon, and the tension in the room was building. Craig Whitaker, one of our Raising the Bar board members, and the person who first saw the contest promotion on line and had suggested that we give it a shot, was a wreck. He and I had spent countless hours together planning and organizing for months, and now we were down to the final two hours.

We decided to take a walk along the waterfront behind the theater to burn off some of our nervous energy. With our adrenalin pumping, the walk seemed more like a jog. We walked and speculated on the outcome. One minute we'd be up, then down, then up again. We had started the contest strong and were in first place for the first two scheduled status reports, then Deluxe announced that Red Wing, Minnesota had taken the lead. The next day Deluxe announced that we were in a dead heat. That was to be the last announcement until the winner was declared, so it was anybody's guess who had won.

Craig, who had spent a lifetime on the technical side of the music and entertainment industry, had the most encouraging observation. Deluxe had informed the five finalists that they would be sending a crew to each of our towns to film the final minutes leading up to the announcement and capture reactions afterward. The production crew was from a company called Flo Nonfiction, out of Austin, Texas. We had gotten to know them from their previous site visits to Bristol when we were competing to become a finalist. Dave Layton, the cinemaphotographer, was originally from Philly and still had family there. He told us upon his arrival that morning that he got to choose which of the five towns he would cover and chose the Bristol assignment so he could also visit his family while he was in the area. The story made sense, but Craig wasn't buying it. Privately he said, "Bill, this is the A team. These are the guys who accompanied Amanda Brinkman on the earlier visit. If Deluxe dispatched five crews across the country, they sent the best one here. I see that as a good sign. I think they're here to cover the winner. I was grasping at straws, and that assessment was fine with me, but still, we just didn't know, and Craig would change his mind three times in the next few minutes-up, down and up again.

The Theater was surrounded by TV vans by the time we returned, their satellite dishes extended for live broadcasts. 3-CBS Philly, 6 ABC, NBC-10, and Fox 29 were all there. It was fun seeing Borough residents doing "man on the street" interviews. We entered the theater and saw that it had filled since we had left. My wife, Karen, who had worked the trenches since we entered the contest, was stressed. She was in charge of checking guests against the list of those who had reserved seats and had gotten some pressure form late arrivals who wanted to get in. She didn't want anyone to miss the event, and I didn't either. I whispered, "Most people are already seated, so just let them in. They'll sort it out once they're inside"

It was approaching the 1:30 start of our program where I was scheduled to speak, and as I worked the crowd, I began to well up inside. These weren't just spectators who'd shown up out of curiosity, they were workers! Kids, parents, grandparents, professionals, cops, firemen, teachers, nurses- I'd known most of them for years, some my entire life. They'd done everything we had asked and more in order to win. I hoped they wouldn't be disappointed.

Mayor Joe Saxton kicked things off with words of welcome. Then he led the crowd in his trade mark cheer we'd done in high school: "We're from Bristol, couldn't be prouder. If you can't hear us, we'll yell a little louder." Sax had them repeat it a few times, and each time they grew louder. Sure, it was hokey, but watching grown adults, some significantly advanced in age, cheer at the top of their lungs was a beautiful thing.

It was my turn to speak. Now, I'm no stranger to microphones and usually welcome any opportunity to address residents. But this was different. We were minutes away from what would either be Bristol's greatest triumph or one of its greatest disappointments, and I didn't know what to say.

I decided to stick with what I'd been thinking since we made the cut to the final five towns. I congratulated them on a tremendous effort. I told them that we might never know the extent to which each of them reached out to friends and relatives across the country or coworkers here at home to vote, but they knew what they did, and had every reason to be proud. I told them it would be great if we won, but if we didn't, we'd still get up the next morning and continue to do what we'd been doing to get us here in the first place: marketing, promoting, working together, pitching in for Historic Bristol Borough.

I panned the audience and so many faces jumped out at me. People who had worked so hard. My family, who put up with the demands of the contest for months. Harry Crohe and Craig Whitaker who literally began every day by calling to ask what they could do to help. Shirley Brady who was a foot soldier throughout, Lorrain Cullen, Justin Saxton, Carl White, Jr., Senator Tommy Tomlinson, John Cordisco, Patrick Mulhern, Kelly Rosado, Michael Crossan, Bridget Shaw, Brian Townsend, Jim Sell, Rosie Torres, and so many more.

I brought Craig Whitaker to the stage to share an idea he had run with. Everyone in the audience had been given a small piece of paper when they arrived and asked to write their feelings at that moment. The papers had been collected and now he produced a Champaign bottle he had decorated the night before. He explained that their notes had been inserted and the bottle corked. He held it up and said it was a bottle of the amazing Bristol spirit. He said we would store it in Mayor Saxton's office and uncork it whenever we needed an emotional boost. It would be our own little time capsule of the experience. Hokey? Not to me, and not to the people in the room.

It was 1:45, time to wrap up. I shared a paraphrased excerpt of Teddy Roosevelt's "Man in the Arena" speech. I took the liberty to substitute the word "town" for "man."

The credit belongs to the town that is actually in the arena, whose face is marred by dust and sweat and blood; who strives valiantly; who errs, who comes short again and again, because there is no effort without error and shortcoming; but who does actually strive to do the deeds; who knows great enthusiasms, the great devotions; who spends itself in a worthy cause; who at the best knows in the end the triumph of high achievement, and who at the worst, if it fails, at least it fails while daring greatly.

I said that we had certainly spent ourselves in a worthy cause and, we had dared greatly. I said that I'd never seen the town more united and determined, and, in that regard we had already won.

It was 1:50 and time to stop. I left the podium and mingled with the crowd. At 1:55 my son Greg, who is a Borough Councilman and who, along with Justin Saxton, had also handled much of our social media presence during the contest, came up to me and said quietly, "Do you want some news?"

"I don't know," I said. "Do I?

He smiled and said, "Do you want some news, or don't you?"

I nodded.

"I was just in the lobby and saw Amanda Brinkman in the parking lot. I'm sure she's not here to tell us we lost."

There it was. We'd won. And soon all of these wonderful people in the room would know as well. Overcome with emotion, I sat down and waited.

At precisely 2:00 PM the screen went live with Amanda's image. All five towns had been told that they would see the announcement simultaneously via a broadcast from New York. She began with a recap of the contest and the process. She congratulated all of the participants and then said, "The 2017 Winner of the Deluxe Corporation's Small Business Revolution is…"

The pre-recorded broadcast continued in the towns of the four other finalists, but at the Bristol location the screen went black. Seconds later, Amanda Brinkman appeared from back stage to make the announcement in person. As she approached the podium and the audience realized what was happening, the room erupted and the noise was deafening. I slumped in my chair and took it all in. People were on the feet, hugging, crying, cheering. It was so loud that Amanda couldn't make herself heard above the crowd for what was at least three minutes. At one point, I saw her wipe a tear from her eye. How great it must be to bring that much joy to people.

When the hoopla subsided Amanda spoke about what a great job we had done to win and what would happen next. I'm not sure anyone in the room really took in the details. It was time to party. We'd deal with the next steps tomorrow.

The crowd lingered after the announcement, and a video crew from Calkins Media did interviews with people in the room. Afterward, I came across one of the interviews on YouTube (https://www.youtube.com/watch?v=VyPj135KwDA) that they did with long-time Borough resident, "Googie" Angelaccio. Googie's birth name is Anthony, but he's been Googie for as long as I've known him. I'm not sure what the origin of the name is. Nicknames are a big thing in Bristol, and you could never trace them all.

Anyway, here's what Googie said that day. "I've been a resident of Bristol for seventy-seven years. I saw the lows, saw the highs when I was a kid. Then the mediocre, and back up now. The town is what it is. Its grown. It's the best. The best small town in the country." The syntax could have been worked on, but the message from the heart was perfect. "The best small town in the country!"

Googie's brother Bobby stood next to him as he spoke. Now Bobby is a bear of a man, affectionately known as having a bit of a tough guy, crusty side to him. But while his brother spoke you could see Bobby wipe a tear from his cheek.

The irony is that Bobby's restaurant, Annabella, so named for his mother, would go on to be one of the six businesses Deluxe would choose for a makeover and be featured in the Small Business Revolution video series. But he didn't know that then. None of us even knew the process Deluxe would eventually use to make their selections. The emotion Bobby and his brother displayed that day had nothing to do with benefits the contest would bring. It was simply about winning. That's what it was for all of us.

In the weeks to come we would be fully immersed in the filmmaking, capital improvements and technical expertise Deluxe would offer our business owners, but at that moment, what mattered most was the total eruption of spirt, pride and renewed confidence in the people of Bristol Borough. The Deluxe Small Business Revolution contest had awakened a sleeping giant, and we were on our way.

Chapter 13- Entering the Contest

We were having another one of our full house exhibit openings at the Centre for the Arts, and I was greeting our guests when I noticed two of our RTB board members, Ron Walker and Craig Whitaker, engaged in serious conversation. Craig's wheels are always turning and you can usually tell from his body language when he's pitching a new idea.

Ron saw me and waved me over. "Craig has an idea he wants to tell you about."

To be honest, my heart sank a little. I'm a sucker for good ideas, and people love to share them with me. The problem is I have trouble walking away once I hear one, and usually end up oversubscribed, trying to do too much at once. The gallery was still fairly new and I was putting in more hours than I had bargained for, not to mention all of the other time consuming Raising the Bar initiatives. So, I'd been working on saying no to new tasks and trying instead to do just a few things well. But Craig's enthusiasm was infectious, so I listened.

"You know the TV guy, Robert Herjavec, from Shark Tank?" Craig asked.

I nodded, not sure where this could possibly be going.

"Did you see his post that's circulating on Facebook?"

I said I hadn't.

"There's a post showing Herjavec's photograph with the caption, 'This man wants to give $500,000 to one small town in America. Why not make it yours?'"

I shrugged. "Probably bogus," I said. "There's a lot of crap on the Internet."

Craig was not deterred. "This is the real thing. There's a link explaining everything. It's sponsored by some company in Minnesota. Deluxe, or something like that. They call it the Main Street- Small Business Revolution. They did it last year and gave a half mill to some town in Indiana. The link lets you download the application to nominate a town. I think we should go for it. I checked it out. They want a five-hundred-word essay and answers to some other questions about the town. Ron and I think you're the guy to do it. They also want a contact person. That should be you too."

I still wasn't convinced it was worth our time. Besides, entering a national contest wasn't on my To Do list when I got up that morning. I promised I'd look at it, but...

By 10:30 that night I was hooked on the concept and busy with the application. When I learned that a town could nominate itself as often as its residents liked, I posted the link on the Raising the Bar Facebook group and invited the three-thousand plus members to join in the application process.

That's when the real story begins. Analysts say it was social media that brought about the Arab Spring in 2011 when thousands of protesters communicating on Facebook and Twitter promoted demonstrations that eventually brought down the governments of Tunisia, Libya, and Egypt, and sparked unrest in a handful of other Arab countries.

Back home, I believe that Raising the Bar's presence on social media was the single most important factor that enabled us to mobilize and empower the wonderful people of Bristol Borough to step up and participate in a positive revolution of our own.

The response on Facebook was strong. A couple of hundred Bristolians "liked" the idea, and several pledged to actually join in the nomination process. One person, sorry to say I don't remember who, wrote that she had already submitted her narrative. I do remember

Beth Angelaccio asking me to look over her application and provide feedback before she sent it in. I did, and her application was great. I know my daughter Leighann also submitted, as did Craig. Beyond that, I just didn't know how many people would actually follow through.

I still didn't think we had a snowball's chance in you know what to win a national contest, but I now felt that the enthusiastic vibe from the town was a good thing for our collective morale and worth rolling with for a while.

After the application deadline closed, a couple of weeks went by, and things died down. It was early fall, and Karen and I were crossing the Burlington-Bristol Bridge on the way home from a drive to the Jersey shore. The speaker phone rang and the caller identified herself as Tanya Shurr Belk, a producer with the Flo Non-Fiction film company out of Austin, Texas. She explained that her company was reviewing the Small Business Revolution applications on behalf of Deluxe Corporation and that Bristol Borough had really caught their attention. I was floored when she said they had received over one hundred applications from the Borough. It was a very emotional thing to learn that the public's response was far greater than I ever imagined. I wish I knew the names of everyone who submitted, because without them, we never would have made it to first base.

"No one else came close to that number," she added. "We're trying to decide which towns will make our short list of eight contestants. Do you have a few minutes to answer some questions?"

Karen and I were silently fist pumping as I pulled over in the Mill Street parking lot and turned off the engine. Tanya and I spoke for almost forty minutes. She peppered me with questions about Bristol's greatest assets, our greatest challenges. Which groups were major players in town? What was the Raising the Bar group all about? She explained that they had received 14,000 nominations from 3500 towns across the country. Their next step would be to narrow the applicants to a short list of eight towns which would each receive a site visit from the Flo Non-Fiction film crew and representatives from Deluxe. At the end of the call, she said she was feeling pretty good about this and we'd hear soon if we'd make the cut.

Soon after we heard the announcement. Bristol Borough was selected as one of the eight short listed towns selected from a crowded national field. Holy *7%#. I thought. This was for real.

The following Monday, I explained the implications to the Borough Council at their monthly meeting. This was a very big deal. The Deluxe/Flo team would travel ten thousand miles to visit all eight towns. They would arrive in Bristol on January 11, (My mother's Birthday which I saw as a good omen) and we'd have three days to convince them to pick us as one of the five finalists before the nationwide on-line voting began.

Obviously, everyone was ecstatic. When I finished my presentation, Council President Ralph DiGuiseppe pledged the full support of council and added, "Bill, if anyone can get us into the finals, it's you. And if we do make it, I know we'll win." Thanks, Ralph. No pressure there.

In 1969, Joe Nameth, quarterback of the New York Jets famously made a bold prediction that his team would defeat the heavily favored Colts in the upcoming Super Bowl. They did, and made history in the process.

The Borough council meetings are televised on the local cable channel. Caught up in the emotion of the moment, I guess I was channeling Broadway Joe when I impulsively said, "Coming this far is an honor, but we're not satisfied. We're in this to win." It was bluster for sure, but given the public's early showing, I was starting to believe it. But things were going to happen fast, and we had our work cut out for us.

Chapter 14- Pick Us!

"Many are the plans in a person's heart, but it is the decision of the LORD that endures." Proverbs 19:21.

I'm no theologian, despite my eight years of studying catechism at St. Ann School in Bristol, nine if you count the broken English version we received from Sister Celina in kindergarten. Maybe that's why I've always struggled with this proverb, the colloquial version of which is, "Man plans and God laughs."

It's not that I don't believe God has a master plan for us, because I do, and, in highly stressful times, I find myself most at peace when I take Karen's advice to "Let go and let God." It's just that I didn't think God was about to show favoritism in the Small Business Revolution contest. Besides, if God was going to weigh in, then I wanted to follow the dictum of most other "type A" personalities: "God helps those who help themselves."

So, as Amanda Brinkman and her team prepared to begin their 10,000-mile journey to select the five finalists, a group of us huddled to figure out how we could help ourselves in the process. Deluxe would spend three days in each town, surveying the landscape and talking to town and civic leaders, business owners and random people on the street. We learned that we would be the second to last town they would visit on a tour that would begin in November and end in mid-January. It felt a little bit like an episode from The Bachelorette, with eight towns waiting to get a Rose. We weren't about to sit back and wait while seven other suitors played virtual kissy-face with Deluxe. We needed a plan, a slogan, something that would engage the whole town long before Deluxe arrived and keep Bristol in the thoughts of Deluxe even as they visited other towns. We needed to make sure that when they picked the five finalists they would pick us.

I remember saying that to the group, and then the lightbulb went on. We'd make "Pick Us!" our slogan. Things exploded from there. We raised more money and had hundreds of Pick US! posters printed with the black and orange SBR logo at the top, a large PICK US! in the middle and the Raising the Bar logo at the bottom. Karen and Shirley Brady visited every shop, restaurant, and professional office on Mill Street to ask owners if they would display the sign. Everyone said yes. We had a large vinyl "Pick Us!" banner strung across the street. We made a Pick Us! graphic that residents used as their Facebook profile picture. We distributed large Pick Us! stickers for people to wear when Deluxe arrived.

Then Craig Whitaker had a great idea. We'd film business owners, town leaders, professionals, waitresses, bartenders, anyone willing. All would have a similar short script. "Hi I'm so and so, and I want to say, "Pick Us!" I scheduled the "talent" and we visited everyone at their place of business where Craig would do then filming. We'd shoot five or ten in a row and Craig's granddaughter, Sydney, would edit them each night and we'd post them on the Raising the Bar Facebook site. Soon people began requesting that we'd film them. When we reached the point where we couldn't keep up with requests, we encouraged people to film and post their own versions. People filmed house parties, family dinners, church groups, classrooms, all with the same, short message. This was Bristol's version of going viral. As we got closer to Christmas we filmed Santa Clause and the Men of Harmony choral group in Dickens attire. The Borough Council interrupted their monthly meeting to say "Pick Us!" in unison. Barbers, hair stylists, construction workers, all paused at their duties to deliver the message.

Looking back, the Pick Us! program energized and focused the town. It would be an easy transition to the voting when the time came, and that was crucial to our success. But the other benefit was equally important. As the Deluxe team traveled from town to town across the country, they were sent an incessant level of Pick Us! messages on Facebook. Each night a new wave of videos would be posted and the

Deluxe team would be tagged in each. Whether they were in Marietta, Ohio; Kingsburg, California, Red Wing, Minnesota or Frostburg, Maryland, they were seeing and hearing from Bristol Borough. We were building anticipation.

Next, we set out to make their arrival special. The film crew from Flo Non-Fiction arrived first and Karen and I planned lunch for them at Cesare's. As always, Donnie Petolillo did an outstanding job. Ron Walker met with the hotel manager and arranged for their rooms to be upgraded. We had obtained the names in advance of those who would be arriving and prepared personalized hospitality bags for each of them, including samples Bristol's own Dad's Hat Whiskey. Each bag contained a personalized binder with copies of forty letters from leaders of Borough organizations amplifying their willingness to do all that was necessary to advance Bristol Borough's candidacy if we were pickled.

When the Deluxe team arrived in town from the hotel, they were greeted by signs in virtually every storefront urging them to Pick Us! That night Raising the Bar hosted them at a cocktail reception at the King George with seventy community leaders. Robert Strasser, Bruce Lowe and Chef Fabian outdid themselves with the spread. We provided all of the Bristol guests with Pick Us! stickers and a photo and profile of each of our Deluxe guests. This allowed our people to engage them on a personal level right away. The overall point was to convey to Deluxe that we pay attention to detail and we would do the same if selected to compete in their contest.

Following the large group reception, a representative group of Raising the Bar board members had a private dinner with the Deluxe team upstairs. No business was conducted. We simply, ate, drank, laughed and bonded. The food was outstanding and the fellowship even better. Ron McGuckin told one humorous and engaging story after another as only Ron can.

Over the next three days, Deluxe would continue to experience the town to evaluate whether we would make the final five. But to paraphrase the famous line from the Jerry McGuire movie, I had a good feeling that we had them at hello.

Chapter 15- The Winning Edge

In 1972 the Miami Dolphins of the NFL made history by posting a perfect undefeated season, winning every regular season game, plus the playoffs and the Super Bowl. It is an achievement that has been unmatched in the 45 years since. During their heralded season, the Dolphins won four of their games by four points or less, beating the Vikings by two, the Jets by four, the Bills by one and the Steelers by four. Following the season, Dolphins coach, Don Shula, wrote a book titled, The Winning Edge. *In it he emphasizes the very fine line that exists between "winning" and "losing," and the importance of preparation, of paying attention to every detail needed for success. In its time, the book was used not only by coaches, but by sales managers and corporate leaders looking for a competitive advantage.*

As I've said, if you want to win at something, it's important to tap into the knowledge of those who know more or have more experience than you. It's also important to know the rules. In Mid-November, as soon as I learned that Bristol Borough was selected as one of the eight shortlisted towns, I started thinking about these two axioms and where I might find answers to the ton of questions swirling in my head. I decided to start by talking to the people in Wabash, Indiana, who had won the contest the previous year.

I googled the Wabash website and found the phone number for Mayor Scott Long. I called and was relieved that I was put right through. I identified myself and said I was calling from Bristol Borough, which had just made the shortlist of towns competing in the Small Business Revolution. I complimented him on Wabash's win and explained that I was Bristol's town representative for this year's contest. I told him I was hoping to gain some insight as to how things worked. He was gracious and said he would put me through to Christine Flohr who had headed up their effort. I had watched the eight-part SBR video series about Wabash and had been impressed by Christine. She was attractive, articulate, knowledgeable and passionate about her town. I learned later that she was also a Cross Fit enthusiast, and that says a lot about her energy level. I was hoping she was also accessible and willing to share some insights.

It turns out she was terrific. My opening question was, "How did you win?" She laughed and we ended up talking for a long time. She reaffirmed much of what we were already planning, but really drove home how important it was to get the schools involved: parents, students, staff, everyone. She also said that Wabash was losing going into the final days before pulling it out. That would prove to be prophetic in our experience as well.

She was explaining the on-line voting process and I asked how soon voting would start after the finalists were announced in February. I was floored to learn that voting would begin on the same day and would only last a week! That phase was almost three months away, and Cameron Potts of Deluxe would eventually explain all of that in detail, but I felt that hearing this now, in mid-November, would give us an important leg up. We all know the sayings, "Do first things first" or "Don't put the cart before the horse." That's normally good advice, but it wouldn't apply here as far as I was concerned. It was clear to me that we needed a parallel effort NOW. We'd launch the Pick Us! campaign AND mobilize our people to prepare to vote. That way, if we made the finals, we would hit the ground running when voting began. We were NOT going to lose a precious day or two of voting later while training people how to vote. We'd be ready on the first day, the first hour. The plan was to take the lead early and never look back. Hopefully, that would be our winning edge.

Chapter 16- Making the Big Dance

The Deluxe announcement of the five finalist towns was scheduled to be live-streamed on the SBR website at 7:00 AM Eastern time on February 9. All of the work on our Pick Us! campaign would come down to that announcement, and my nerves were shot. I hadn't slept much and my original thought was to stay in bed with a pillow over my head and let someone tell me how things turned out, but Karen wouldn't have it. She ordered me out of bed and I complied.

It was 6:30 and I was groggy. Deluxe had chosen the 7:00 AM announcement time to capture the morning shows of the New York media market. I thought briefly of the people in Kingsburg, California, another one of the shortlisted towns, who would need to be sitting by their computers at 4:00 AM Pacific time if they wanted to hear their fate live. I was glad I lived on the East Coast.

Fortunately, Craig Whitaker called at 6:45 to shoot the breeze and kill the time until the announcement. I'm glad he did because as I booted our computer I realized in true Murphy's Law fashion that it had chosen that morning to go off line. The minutes ticked away as I scrambled to reset my modem, and I asked Craig to stay on the phone in case I couldn't connect in time. I didn't, and Craig gave me a play by play as the announcement began.

"Ok, there's Amanda," he said. "Here we go."

There was silence and I said, "What's going on?"

"She's reviewing what the SBR contest is all about."

I gave up on my computer and decided to just listen to Craig. "Tell me what's happening!" I shouted.

"Still general stuff about the contest," he said. The he added, "Hold on, here we go."

I waited.

"False alarm. She and Robert are talking about all the miles they traveled and how Robert liked the food in the different towns."

We waited and then it happened.

Those who were around on May 6, 1974 will always remember the celebrated call of Philadelphia Flyers announcer, Gene Hart, in the final seconds of game seven of the Stanley Cup playoffs, when he said in rising decibels, "The Flyers win the Stanley Cup! The Flyers win the Stanley Cup! The Flyers have won the Stanley Cup!" I still get chills when I hear reruns of the call.

I had that flashback when Craig finally shouted, "We made it! We made it! Bristol Borough is the first one in. We made it!" I could hear his wife, Lynn, celebrating in the background and Karen was pounding on my back. It was a Gene Hart type moment, and it was all good.

I was glad that my computer was off line that morning, because I got to share the moment with Craig. What most people didn't know was that Craig was undergoing successful treatment for prostate cancer during the contest and wasn't able to drive the long distances he usually traveled to make his sales calls. The contest had been a good distraction for him, and he had done a terrific job.

I'd had a casual acquaintance with Craig for forty years, but you can really bond with someone when you work hard together toward a common goal. We still had work to do, and it felt good knowing we'd do it together.

After the hoopla died down we learned that North Adams, Massachusetts; Red Wing Minnesota; Georgetown, South Carolina, and Kingsburg, California were the other finalists.

The final phase of the SBR contest was here. Nationwide on-line voting would begin immediately and last for one week until February 16. Up until this point decisions about who made the shortlist and then, who were the finalists, were completely in the hands of the Deluxe team. I think we had done outstanding work in wooing Deluxe during the entire process and it had paid off. But now, the subjectivity was out of the equation. The winner would be based not on Deluxe's evaluation of the towns, but on actual votes cast. Our fate was solely in our hands, and for the first time, I felt really, really good. We were ready.

Chapter 17- Eight Days in February

Calls started coming in from family, friends and Raising the Bar members wanting to share the moment. I saw a call from Peg Quann of the Bucks County Courier-Times and took it right away. We had agreed to talk as soon as the announcement was made. I had already prepared two quotes, one if we made the cut and one if we didn't. I was happy to deliver the former. Throughout the week of voting, calls from any of the media outlets: The *Courier-Times, Bucks County Advance*, the Philadelphia *Inquirer, LevittownNow*, the *Bristol Times*, the television and radio stations in Philly, all would take precedence over any other call. I could "talk" to almost four thousand people at once using our Raising the bar Facebook group, but *the media could talk to tens of thousands at once, and I would not miss any opportunity to get our word out.*

The joy of those first few minutes after the announcement would turn into eight of the most exhausting, tension filed, emotionally charged days in memory. Before it was over we'd experience confidence, hope, discouragement, rumors, accusations, technical difficulties, and some amazing displays of grace and sportsmanship from all of the competing towns in the face of fierce competition. I'm tracing the events of those eight days here to acknowledge the work of so many people, and to provide a game plan for networking and organization for the next generation of Bristol's leaders who will have their own projects to pursue.

I'm convinced that some of the negative distractions we experienced would have knocked us off our game were it not for the organizational structure we had in place. I have been involved in sixteen political campaigns as a primary player, four of my own, two for my son Greg and ten for state representative Tom Corrigan. The record in those campaigns was 16-0 and the fundamentals of organization were not lost this time. Do things well in advance. Have your photos and graphics ready. Prepare your literature for printing early. Build and mobilize your network early, and define your message, early. We'd been working on all of that for over a month and we were ready.

Chapter 18- Paul Revere's Ride

As kid's, most of us may remember the poem, Paul Revere's Ride, by Longfellow.

"Listen my children, and you shall hear
Of the midnight ride of Paul Revere,
On the 18th of April in seventy-five;
Hardly a man is now alive
Who remembers that famous day and year…"

Longfellow goes on for thirteen stanzas to describe Paul Revere's famous ride, alerting the militiamen of Lexington and Concord of the arrival of the British troops in Boston, setting the stage for the dramatic confrontation at Lexington Green where the "Shot heard 'round the world" would be fired.

His warning of the British arrival wasn't a haphazard, spur-of- the-moment act of patriotism. Longfellow devotes the next two stanzas to explain the detailed plans that had been set to alert the colonists. Once Revere saw the lantern in the Old North Church, he knew it was his cue to make his ride. And the patriots, hearing the shouts of "To arms, to arms, the Redcoats are coming" as Revere galloped by in the middle of the night, knew it wasn't some nut letting off steam after having one too many Samuel Adams beers. It was part of the plan. The colonists had prepped for it, and now it was time to act.

In case you missed it, the colonists went on to win the revolution. There is a parallel story here about how we prepared during the previous two months so that major organizations in Bristol Borough and surrounding areas had been solicited, prepped, reminded, begged, and hounded to be poised like the minutemen at Lexington and Concord, to begin on-line voting the moment we learned that we had made the finals. Again, in case you missed it, we went on to win a revolution of our own- the Deluxe Small Business Revolution!

The rules were one vote per computer devise, per browser, per day. Our goal was to reach out to organizations with multiple computers and lots of people to use them. We printed flyers and cards with our call to action, explaining the rules and asking everyone to vote each day on every computer device and to reach out to friends and family to do the same. Then we hit the organizations.

Chapter 19- The Pep Rally

We began the week with a pep rally at the Goodwill Hose #3 Fire company's banquet hall. In true Bristol fashion, over three hundred people showed up, including our state legislators; the local head of AFSCME, Kevin Burns, President of the Ancient Order of Hibernians; elected officials from surrounding towns like Bobby Harvie from Falls, Tom Tosti from Middletown Township, and others. Mayor Joe DiGirolamo of Bensalem Township, couldn't come but pledged his enthusiastic support. We also had local councilmen Ralph DiGuiseppe, Greg Pezza, Lou Quattrocchi, Lorraine Cullen, Tony Riccio, Betty Rodriguez and Mayor Joe Saxton on hand. Paul Gosline and Dave Albright graciously opened the doors of the beautifully renovated firehall to us. RTB Board member, Mycle Gorman, donated hundreds of bottles of water and soft pretzels. He and Ron McGuckin were leaving shortly for a national business conference in Cancun where Ron would be the principle presenter. They were bummed about not being in town for part of the week of voting. I'd learn later that Ron began each of his daily conference presentations by instructing his audience to take out their cell phones and vote for Bristol.

I spoke to the crowd and gave them a big dose of rah, rah. I also cautioned them not to become complacent and to absolutely play by the rules. Cameron Potts is Vice President of Public Relations and Community Management at Deluxe, which was a pretty big deal. He had set up a conference call with the community leaders from each of the five towns to review the rules. We were allowed to vote once per day per device and Deluxe reserved the right to disqualify any town that violated the rules by using BOT software or similar programs which basically programmed a computer to vote robotically over and over. He also explained that their system had a way of knowing when people were voting more often than allowed, and those votes were automatically discounted at their end.

I reminded the crowd of the story of a Chicago Cubs fan, whose interference with a foul ball in the eighth inning of Game 6 of the 2003 National League Championship Series, was a contributing factor in the Cubs losing the game and eventually the series. I always thought he got a raw deal, but nevertheless, the poor guy went through hell in Chicago. I urged those present not to become the person who would be remembered forever as the one who got us disqualified from this contest. "We've got a tremendous machine in place," I said. "We've led in every category to get to this point and we're going to win. PLAY BY THE RULES."

I had asked Craig to que up a video clip we prepared. It was hokie, but I wanted to do it. It was a scene from Rocky II. Adrian had just given birth after a difficult delivery, and Rocky was at her hospital bedside. Rocky was training for another fight with Apollo Creed, and he knew Adrian hated his fighting. Caught up in the emotion of seeing their new baby and a weakened Adrian, he told her that maybe he'd give up fighting if that was what she wanted. Adrian asked him to lean in closer and whispered, "Win," and then repeated it louder, "Win!" The scene cuts to the stirring Bill Conti composition of the Rocky theme while we see Rocky train. Damn, hokie or not, I love that scene and get chills every time I see it. We left the hall that night charged up, united, and knowing what we had to do.

RTB member, Carl White, Jr., had helped design our promotional graphics: posters, table tents and business sized cards with reminders of how and when to vote. We raised money and printed over twenty thousand pieces! We distributed them to our core committee in stacks of one-hundred with the reminder that they did us no good unless they ended up in voter's hands. We also made digital files for use on Facebook and in email broadcasts. I wrote literature describing what was at stake and the kind of help we were looking for. Each media outlet or organization would require that information, and it was vital to have it in advance. *Again, because people could vote once a day, the plan was to lose NO TIME once the voting began.*

Within minutes of the announcemt that we'd made the finals, hundreds of people were able to change their Facebook profile picture to a "vote for Bristol Borough Feb. 9-16" with the web address below it.

From the outset, we decided we would wage this effort on two levels. Our team would reach out to every family to get their relatives, neighbors and coworkers to vote. *But a small group of us would focus on cultivating those groups or individuals who could influence hundreds of votes at a time.*

20- The Big Players

We had our full machine in operation within minutes of the announcement. Below is just a sampling of those exceptional efforts and the people who led them. The list is long and is my best effort to include everyone. I apologize in advance for anyone I've missed. It was a crazy week.

THE SCHOOLS

Bristol Borough Schools

Taking Christine's advice from Wabash, we wanted to ensure that the schools were fully on board. The Bristol Borough School district had hundreds of computers, and we wanted to make sure that each was used for voting each day. We contacted **Superintendent of schools, Tom Shaffer and Principal Kelly Rosado,** and both couldn't have been more cooperative. But we knew that grass roots, personal contact of teachers and other key institutional people is what would make things work. **Heather Quattrocchi** was extremely helpful in the high school as was **Michael Crossan** in the Snyder-Girotti elementary school. **Patrick Mulhern** helped distribute our flyers to the schools to be sent home with the students to enlist their parents. **Bethann Olczak, Shea Cialella, and Kathleen Lochel** helped enlist the PTA.

Conwell-Egan Catholic High School

Brian Townsend had been a friend for years. He had recently been inducted into the Conwell-Egan Catholic High School Basketball Hall of Fame and engaged in fund raising for the school. I asked him to help get CEC on board and he set up a luncheon meeting with **Bill Burns**, an administrator at the school. I asked Craig Whitaker to meet with them. The result was that Burns made an address over the public-address system every day urging kids to vote. They also sent our flyers home to the parents. Conwell-Egan is in Levittown, but several very popular and high-achieving kids from Bristol went to school there. I'm convinced that their classmates and teachers got on board out of respect for the brothers and sisters of the **Konnovitch, Corrigan, Dougherty and Smith families.** It says a lot about the spirit de corps of the school.

St. Mark School

My wife, Karen, is the former principal of St. Mark Catholic School in Bristol. She approached the current principal, **Maria Sanson**, for help and Maria readily agreed and **Bridget Ennis-Shaw,** a borough resident and a teacher at St. Mark's, carried the ball.

Lower Bucks County Chamber of Commerce

Amy McKenna had recently been named executive director of the Lower Bucks County Chamber of Commerce. I had pitched the idea that a victory for Bristol Borough in a contest focused on business development would be a victory for the entire chamber. We needed the chamber's help in reaching out to their members throughout the lower end of the county. **Justin Saxton**, one of our RTB board members and also a member of the chamber, drove home the same message. Amy and her board jumped in with both feet, sending almost daily e-broadcasts to their membership.

Lower Bucks County Hospital

Linda Grass was the executive director of Prime Health Care Lower Bucks Hospital, one of the largest employers in the area. She had proven herself to be very community oriented. She accepted our request and responded with frequent messages to the entire staff. **Sam DeFrancisco** is another community oriented member of the hospital staff and a dynamo of energy and personality. He is one of those foot soldiers you need in any project. He visited every nurses station and department in the hospital urging them to vote and leaving them instructions.

St. Mary Medical Center

St. Mary Medical Center is another major employer in the county. Bristol resident, **Sue Monte,** was a long-time administrator at the center almost fifteen miles away. She had since semi-retired, but I called her anyway to enlist her help and she readily agreed. Like Sam at Lower Bucks, she did the legwork to distribute the cards and place table tent advertisements wherever she was able.

Rotary-Lions-Elks

The social-service clubs in the Borough were in full swing. RTB members **Joanna Schneyder** and **Jim Sell** are officers in the Bristol Rotary. They enlisted the support if their membership and reached out to the network of Rotary clubs throughout the county. **Ron Walker**, another RTB board member and long-time leader in the Bristol Lions club did the same. **Rich Russo, Kelly Bellerby** and the rest of the Bristol Elks leadership reached out to the Elks Club network throughout Pennsylvania.

Visit Bucks

The Bucks County Tourist Commission, commonly known as Visit Bucks, has a vast network of restaurants, shops, hotels, wineries, parks and other visitor attractions throughout the county. **Jerry Lepping**, its executive director, has always been a big supporter of Bristol Borough. He agreed that tourism would certainly receive a significant boost if one of our towns won a national contest. He reached out to their membership on a regular basis.

Bucks County Community College

Bucks County Community College has hundreds of full and part-time faculty and staff and ten thousand full and part-time students. The Lower Bucks campus is little more than a mile from the Borough, and its **Executive Director, Jim Sell**, led the charge to mobilize the campus to vote for Bristol. He also did an excellent job of ensuring that every device in the college was used to vote each day. **Jim and his wife Kelly**, are examples of the growing number of people in the area who are rediscovering Bristol Borough and making it their home.

D & L

The sixty-mile long Delaware Canal is a national landmark that runs south from Easton to Bristol Borough, with a network of loyal enthusiasts in every town it intersects. We contacted **Elissa Garafalo**, Executive Director of the Delaware-Lehigh National Heritage Corridor, for help. She responded by including our effort in the corridor's e-newsletter and urging support.

Our Government Partners

Traditionally, Bristol Borough is a working class, democratic town, and the entire borough council and school board is comprised of democrats. But when it comes to county, state and federal politics, our town leaders, under the leadership of Council President **Ralph DiGuiseppe,** have wisely charted a bi-partisan course of supporting whoever provides effective service for the Borough, especially in assisting with municipal grant applications. **Former Congressman Mike Fitzpatrick, Republican State Senator Tommy Tomlinson, Democratic State Representative, John Galloway and County Commissioner Rob Loughery** for us. Our relationship, skillfully cultivated by Ralph, is a good one. I also had strong relationships with the same players from my years of working for Democratic Representative Tom Corrigan. So, we had little hesitation in approaching all of them for support. The result was an inspiring bi-partisan effort to mobilize their networks to support tiny Bristol Borough.

We knew that public officials and celebrities could have a big impact by promoting the contest on social media, so we put on a full court press. Newly elected **Congressman Brian Fitzpatrick, State Senator Tommy Tomlinson and State Representative John Galloway** agreed to make videotaped messages that they shared with their large networks of followers. In a true display of neighborly spirit, nearby **Representatives Tina Davis, Gene DiGirolamo, and Frank Farry** also taped messages. Once again, our prior planning payed off because we were quickly able to provide their staffs with written content about the contest, a skeletal script they could adapt to their wishes and graphics they could post on their Facebook pages.

County Commissioner **Rob Loughery** was excited about Bristol Borough making the short list and invited me to a public commissioners' meeting in Doylestown. Karen and I made the drive and I was floored to see that Rob had prepared a PowerPoint describing the background of the contest, the voting procedure and our request for official help. He explained that we had a high expectation of making the final five and wanted people to begin voting the very day we were eligible. **Commissioner Chairman, Charlie Martin**, embraced the idea and instructed his staff to do whatever was appropriate to mobilize the vast network of county employees and agencies to get on board. We left with our spirits soaring. Raising the Bar member **Harry Crohe** and his brother Donnie had a wonderful relationship with Commissioner Martin and no doubt their prior lobbying helped.

By now you may be thinking this list is a bit long and you're right. But we're talking about winning a national contest, and I want to make sure that as many players as possible get recognized for their contribution. I also what to ensure that young people in Bristol will have a better understanding about networking and organization when we pass the baton to them as future leaders. So, back to the narrative.

John Cordisco

Bristol native John Cordisco is a remarkable success story. Coming from a blue-collar family of modest means, he grew up on Lincoln Avenue in the heart of the most Italian section of town. Following high school, he went to work as a steelworker while putting himself through Rider College. He then completed his law degree at Temple University at night. He was elected to the Bristol Borough School Board at the age of twenty-two and at twenty-five became one of Pennsylvania's youngest State Representatives. He was a founding partner of the Cordisco and Saile, LLC law firm and became Chairman of the Democratic party of Bucks County, where he developed personal relationships with prominent federal and state democratic officials.

John now lives in the more affluent New Hope area of Bucks County, but I knew his heart and roots remained in Bristol Borough. I called, and he pledged his support. Armed with our digital literature and graphics, he reached out to every democratic committee person in Bucks County to help his hometown.

Bucks County Courier-Times

Earlier in the contest I contacted **Guy Petroziello** editorial page editor of the Courier-Times, to ask for editorial support. He invited me to meet with the editorial board. I invited Craig to come along. We said that last year's winner, Wabash, Indiana with a population of just over 10,000 won the two-way contest in which 180,000 votes were cast. They obviously had help from their surrounding area and we would need the same. We explained everything we had planned to garner that help, but a plug from the paper would go a long way, especially since this year's contest would have five finalists. I proposed a partnership, a kind of joint project to promote the vote. They weren't ready to go that far, but they did invite me to write a seven-hundred-word guest editorial, which I did, and it is reprinted here.

A Vote for Bristol Borough is a Vote for Small Town America

By Bill Pezza

A Vote for Bristol Borough is a Vote for Small Town America

After years of dormancy, small town main streets across the country are experiencing a resurgence, and many nostalgic observers are cheering them on as they rediscover their charm and potential as dining and entertainment centers and more. Chief among their supporters is Deluxe Corporation of Shoreview, Minnesota. The office supply and business services company is making a heroic effort to launch what it calls the main street Small Business Revolution. The company is committed to drawing attention to small town businesses by sponsoring a highly competitive national contest that awards the winning town with a $500,000 business district infusion and an eight-part cable and on-line video series that features their revival. After receiving 14,000 nominations nation-wide, Deluxe informed us that Historic Bristol Borough, Bucks County, is one of eight shortlisted towns still in contention and the only town in Pennsylvania and the tri state area. Thus, we see our candidacy as a wonderful opportunity to showcase not only Bristol Borough, but Bucks County as well.

Last year's winner, Wabash, Indiana, has a population of 11,000. Yet they were able to win in a contest that saw 180,000 votes cast. They obviously did so with the help of good -willed neighbors in their region. Bristol Borough is asking its friends across the county to provide the same kind of help.

Our region is blessed with so many wonderful small towns like Yardley, Newtown, Morrisville, Doylestown, New Hope, Langhorne and others too numerous to mention. Together, we can send a message that Bucks County is a harmonious place with people of good will who value places like Hulmville, Pendel, Tullytown, and, in this case, Bristol Borough, and applaud each other's success.

We've already begun the process of reaching out for support in the region and are heartened by the response. The Bucks County commissioners passed a resolution on February 1 endorsing our effort and encouraging county employees and residents in general to vote for Bristol Borough. Congressman Brian Fitzpatrick, Senator Tommy Tomlinson, State Representatives John Galloway, Tina Davis and Frank Farry have pledged their help via their social media networks. Tourist promoter, Visit Bucks County, as well as the Lower Bucks and Central Bucks Chambers of Commerce are appealing to their members as well as several corporations that are reaching out to their customer bases. Bucks County Community College is reaching out to staff and students. Service cubs like the Bristol Rotary and Bristol Lions are soliciting the help of their county wide sister organizations. Social-service groups like the Ancient Order of Hibernians, the Elks and Loyal Order of the Moose are contacting their membership and fellow lodges in the region. School groups, church groups and scout troops are on board. The Bristol Riverside Theater is reaching out to its subscribers. The movement is also gaining traction with individuals. Hundreds of Bucks residents have generational roots in Bristol Borough and are offering to help their "home town." Large employers like Lower Bucks Hospital and groups affiliated with St. Mary's are joining in. The response has buoyed our already heightened spirits.

We will learn shortly if we will move from the final eight to the final four towns eligible for voting. Because of the nature of the challenge, we have no choice but to proceed now as if we will be selected and we are cautiously optimistic. While the selection of finalists eligible for voting is largely subjective, there are some indicators, and by every empirical social media measure, we are far in front of all of our competitors. When that final announcement comes, and we believe it will, we want to hit the ground running with all of our supporters voting on the day voting begins on February 9 and continuing through February 16 by going to the site www.smallbusinessrevolition.org . Voters are permitted AND ENCIOURAGED to vote once per day per device: computer, lap top, iPad, notebook, smart phone, etc. Anyone in the country may vote. Please reach out to your networks, and friends and relatives far and wide.

Some might say it is risky for Bristol Borough to go out on a limb like this when the outcome is not certain, but to paraphrase Teddy Roosevelt, we're spending ourselves in a worthy cause; from which at best, we will know the triumph of high achievement and at the worst, if we fail, at least we will fail while daring greatly. But with your help, we will succeed.

Remember to vote at www.smallbusinessrevolution.org every day from February 9 to 16. Let's bring this honor home to Bristol Borough and all of Bucks County.

They graciously used it, and it received wide exposure. Moving forward, I got the impression that the more we demonstrated that we weren't just looking for a handout, that we were actually doing everything possible from our end, the more extensive their coverage became. As I've said, we couldn't have won it without the exposure they gave to the effort.

WBCB Radio

I also appeared twice as a noontime guest on WBCB radio's Speak Your Piece program. The station serves Lower Bucks County, and the show's host, **Patricia Wandling,** became one of our most spirited supporters.

We knew that public officials and celebrities could have a big impact by promoting the contest on social media, so we put on a full court press. Newly elected Congressman Brian Fitzpatrick, State Senator Tommy Tomlinson and State Representative John Galloway agreed to make videotaped messages that they shared with their large networks of followers. In a true display of neighborly spirit, nearby Representatives Tina Davis, Gene DiGirolamo and Frank Farry also taped messages. Once again, our prior planning payed off because we were quickly able to provide their staffs with written content about the contest, a skeletal script they could adapt to their wishes and graphics they could post on their Facebook pages.

Jeff Manto

While the political endorsements went well, the search for celebrity endorsements wasn't as easy, but we kept at it. Craig Whitaker got his neighbor, local baseball hero and former Major League player, Jeff Manto, to film a video. The bat that Jeff used to hit four consecutive home runs is in the Baseball Hall of Fame at Cooperstown, NY.

Christopher Gattelli

Bristol native, Christopher Gattelli, won a Tony Award for his choreography of the popular Broadway play, *Newsies.* His father and I played football together at Bristol High and were in each other's wedding. He had since passed away, but I contacted Chris's mom, Dee, who had moved to Virginia to be close to her grandchildren and her daughter. I made the pitch and the next thing we knew, Chris was in a studio in New York filming a video for Facebook, urging not only his hometown fans to vote for Bristol, but his entire Broadway network.

Chris wasn't our only Broadway figure to lend his support. In high school **Ryan O'Gara** worked at the Bristol Riverside Theater where, under their mentoring, he took an interest in stage lighting. He majored in it in college and went on to land positions on Broadway where he did lighting for many major shows including our personal favorite, *Hamilton.* He's a great guy, very popular in town. Ryan's Aunt Patty was Karen's closest childhood friend. Karen called her and bingo, we had another endorsement.

We'll never know how much voting impact these local celebrity videos had. But they certainly boosted the town's spirit each time another appeared on Facebook that week. *They also were a heartwarming reminder about how lasting small-town relationships were. Win or lose, that meant a lot.*

Merrill Reese

Still, we needed bigger guns, and we pushed on. President Lyndon Johnson, the big ol' Texan, used to describe some people he valued as someone you'd *go to the well with*, meaning, when you're pinned down in a long wild west shootout and you needed to get to the well for water, you wanted someone dependable by your side, someone who gets things done. I'm not sure why it's that important to go to a well in the middle of a shootout, but I'm not a Texan. Anyway, Harry Crohe is the kind of person you'd want to go to the well with. He was a rock-solid foot soldier throughout the contest. A former President of the Bucks County Rescue Squad, he was used to being a public servant. As we scratched our heads thinking about celebrities we could approach, he said he had a personal relationship with Merrill Reese, the radio voice of the Philadelphia Eagles. Merrill is an icon in the Delaware Valley and is also Vice President of WBCB radio. When Harry approached him, and explained what he needed, Merrill readily agreed and made a fantastic broadcast as only Merrill can. We posted his video message all over Facebook and it went viral.

Speaking of Harry, he Brought Scott Bahner from the rescue squad on board, and Scott, together with people like Chief Herb Slack,

Emergency management Director, Merle Winslow, Tony Bucci, and Rosie Torres did an outstanding job in reaching out to the fire services and first responders throughout the county.

WMMR Radio

Craig Whittaker contacted the morning show team of Preston and Steve on WMMR radio, a highly rated rock station in Philadelphia. They offer an entertaining mix of comedy and music, and embraced Bristol's candidacy so much that they made it a part of their daily routine that week. It even reached the point that they jokingly began claiming that our anticipated win would be attributed to them. It was fun and we loved the coverage.

WFAN Radio

Mike Missanelli hosts the afternoon drive spot on WFAN, 97.5, a major sports talk radio station in Philadelphia. He is a graduate of Bristol high school and a member of their 1975 state championship basketball team. He went on to play baseball at Penn state. He no longer lives in town but still bleeds Bristol's red and gray colors. There is no doubt he would have helped us were he not on medical leave, recovering from surgery to relieve a painful back condition. He was a longtime friend of John Cordisco, and I called John to see if he could use his connection to Mike to get some quality time on the show with the guest host. He did, and gave us a good plug. I called in a day later and repeated the message for morning host, Anthony Gargano and his guest Brian Baldinger. Baldinger is a former player for the Philadelphia Eagles and an NFL analyst. I loved Baldinger's work and knew these guys often reacted to life on a visceral level and I took that approach. Knowing it was a sports talk show, I told them that Bristol's role in this contest is like Rocky Balboa and Hoosiers rolled into one. This was a small-town, down-on-its-luck underdog taking a shot at the big prize, and we'd have to claw our way to the top. They bought in big time. In fact, Gargano gave his trademark, "This is awesome," response and asked me to repeat the voting process. Both urged their listeners to help us out. Again, we can't be sure how many votes were generated by these contacts, but they certainly energized our supporters and kept the positive buzz going. We wanted everyone to stay on the bandwagon.

Bristol Expatriates

There was one more important group that would contribute to our effort, and I came to call them the expatriates, people who had been born and raised in Bristol Borough but had emigrated out of town for a variety of reasons. Some had followed their jobs. Some had retired and moved South seeking better weather. Others had left after getting married and finding a home elsewhere because it may have been the fashionable thing to do at the time. The one thing they all had in common is that their hearts always remained in Bristol, and it seemed the older they got the more nostalgic they became for their hometown.

A case in point is Joe Lelinski. Joe and I played football together in high school and went on to become fraternity brothers in college. Our fathers worked together at the Owens-Illinois box factory in Croydon, and Joe and I spent our college summers working the midnight shift at the same place. Joe got married and became one of those guys looking for a new home, and settled in Falls Township. I'd see Joe and his wife Mary occasionally and we were friends on Facebook, but when the SBR contest hit, he resurfaced in a big way. Most notably, he reached out to our network of hundreds of fraternity brothers to enlist their support. I am a former president of Mu Alpha Kappa, and the fraternity keeps an extensive e-mail base. Joe utilized that base every day to remind our brothers to vote. Their response was heartwarming. The point is that Joe is just one of hundreds of Bristolians who had moved away but stepped up enthusiastically to support their hometown. One person wrote from Florida that she was getting her entire retirement community to vote for us.

Chapter 21- Voting Tensions Build

We were running on all cylinders, but we couldn't relax. I'd spent a lifetime urging people to vote on election day, and it wasn't always easy. But this time, we needed people to sustain their voting effort for eight days! They needed to vote on day one, then day two, then day three... The standard greeting in Bristol Borough that week changed from "Hello" to "Did you vote?"

For all of the organizational benefits of Facebook, it certainly has its downside. You may have noticed that some people post flat out stupid things. In the case of the SBR contest, it seems that every community had people who fashioned themselves as computer geniuses who bragged that they could beat the system by voting more often than the rules allowed. This obviously created tension between the communities. Cameron Potts is Vice President of Public Relations and Community Management for Deluxe Corporation, which is a pretty big deal. He was the point person for the voting aspect of the contest and had established a type of hotline the five community leaders could call. I checked in with him frequently and his message was consistent. Deluxe is a multimillion dollar corporation with a massive technology department. They were quite comfortable with their ability to filter out votes that shouldn't have been registered. Despite that, he asked that each of the five community representatives reiterate the rules on Facebook and ask our supporters to stay in line. It's hard to control the boasts of a few uninformed knuckle heads when thousands of people are posting across the country. We fully understood Cam's point and we all agreed. I also reminded him that I had a videotape of myself instructing our team to play by the rules early on at a public rally. Cameron had a tough job. We all did, and we were doing the best we could.

I don't want to give the impression that it was all tension between the towns. There were hundreds of gracious posts from wonderful people throughout the week, like this one by Erin Elise, from North Adams, Massachusetts who wrote, *I finally sat down and watched the videos for the other 4 towns. Wow. It's amazing how similar our stories are and the struggles we share. I wish we could all win, that we could all be in this together and support each other because lord knows, WE ALL NEED this. Best of luck to each town and your beloved supporters! #MyNorthAdams.*

Deluxe set up the contest so that results would only be posted on two days, February 12 and again on the 14th. They would not post results during the last two days of the contest. "Going dark" as the concept was called, was designed to increase anxiety and increase participation.

We waited for the February 12 announcement and were thrilled by what we saw. SBR posted the standings which showed Bristol Borough in first, Red Wing Minnesota second, and North Adams, Massachusetts third. There were high fives all around the room. The approach was working and our people were believing.

In addition to posting the standings, SBR wrote, "UPDATE: Here are the standings after the first three days of voting. Hint: the race is tight and it's still anyone's game. Voting is open through 2/16 - keep up the momentum and spread the word! Your favorite small town could be featured on the #smallbusinessrevolution Main Street."

There was no shortage of opinions that week. More than one person told me they thought we were running away with it and that the reference to a tight race was merely an attempt to bolster the spirts of the other four towns and keep them voting. That was the last thing I wanted to hear. We posted on Facebook how important it was to not become complacent. In fact, we asked everyone to INCREASE their efforts.

We received more good news that day. We had previously heard that Red Wing had enlisted the support of Minnesota United States Senators, Al Franken and Amy Klobuchar. John Cordisco, a Bristol native and currently Chairman of the Bucks County Democratic Party, had been working on getting Democratic Pennsylvanian Governor Tom Wolf or former Governor Ed Rendell to make a video for us. It turned out that Cordisco hit a home run, two actually, as both men made videos for us to post on Facebook, in fact, Governor Wolf's office circulated his throughout the state. Since our geographically closest competitor was in Massachusetts, it made sense to appeal to statewide pride to vote for Bristol Borough.

Things were going VERY well as we worked our way toward the next and final announcement scheduled for February 14. That announcement came as a big Valentine's Day kiss on the lips. *The announcement read: Bristol Leading on the morning of the 14th*

SBR UPDATE: Here are the standings as of 10am this morning. There are three days to go, more than 350,000 total votes have been cast, and it is a VERY. TIGHT. RACE. Now is the time to kick it into high gear and keep those votes rolling in - it's still anybody's game!

I can't describe how proud I was with that news. From back in the fall when our citizens nominated Bristol in runaway fashion, to the literal flood of #mybristolborough postings during the shortlist period, until now with the on-line voting, Bristol had led in every category at every stage. I knew our spirits would be soaring and the other towns had to be a bit deflated. If we kept our shoulder to the wheel, we would bring this home.

For as long as I can remember, Karen and I have celebrated every Valentine's Day at the King George II Inn. We prefer the tavern and always reserve the first booth by the piano player. Karen asked me to request "On My Own," from *Les Miserables*. So, I dropped a couple of bucks in the tip jar, and he played beautifully. Chef Fabian's meal was wonderful as always, and the co-owner, Robert Strasser, bought us an after-dinner drink. One couple stopped by the table to introduce themselves. They were from Levittown and said they recognized me from the SBR promo video. The woman said she wanted us to know that her mother was originally from Bristol, on Swain Street, and they had been voting for us every day. She added that her son was in the army, stationed in South Korea, and he was having his unit vote.

It was so good to unwind. I'd been wired for a week. Make that a month. Actually, make that four months. But things were falling into place. I still worried a little about complacency, but relaxed each time I checked Facebook. Our residents and friends were exploding with excitement and cheering each other on. Everyone was voting.

That was February 14. On the morning of February 15, I was greeted with a hard punch to the stomach that almost took my breath away. Craig called to ask if I'd seen the latest standings posted by SBR. I hadn't. He said that Red Wing, Minnesota had taken the lead.

"That must be a bogus post. Someone is fooling around," I said. "Deluxe already posted the last standings yesterday, before going dark. There's no more postings until they announce the winner."

"I know the rules," Craig said. "But I'm looking at it. Check it out. It's for real.

I did, and this time it was like getting punched in the stomach and then kneed in the face when I doubled over. The post read:

UPDATE: We have a new leader in the clubhouse. After nearly a full week of the standings remaining the same, Red Wing has narrowly moved into the lead today. This contest remains very, very tight across the rankings. And as last year taught us - It is still anyone's game. Voting closes tomorrow at 9 p.m. EST, so be sure to VOTE and SHARE with your friends and family!

New leader in the friggin' clubhouse!!! Are you kidding me? I didn't know what bothered me more, the news that we'd fallen behind or the fact that Deluxe posted another standing update contrary to their guidelines. This would energize the Red Wing voters and possibly poke a hole in our balloon. All of the tension, anxiety and fatigue of the previous months came to the surface. I wanted to punch the wall, but Karen gets mad at me when I do that.

Then it got worse as the phone calls rolled in. People love conspiracy theories. Neil Armstrong never walked on the moon; it was a hoax. The United States blew up the World Trade Center to justify War against Iraq. Charles Lindberg staged a kidnapping story for publicity. Some will believe anything, like Donald Trump is actually a good...never mind.

Anyway, in true conspiracy fashion one friend called and said, "You're getting screwed, Billy. I knew they would never let Bristol win. It's fixed." I thought of the time when John McCain was running for president against Barack Obama and an elderly female supporter at a town hall meeting said Obama was a Muslim. "No Mam," McCain had said as he pulled the microphone away. "That's not true."

That was my response to my friend. I had no doubt of the integrity of the people running the contest. I'd grown to like them a lot. His retort was. "You're being naïve, Billy. It's a shame. You worked hard."

The next call was more of the same. "Listen, I knew the fix was in the day I found out that Red Wing was just a few miles from the Deluxe Corporate headquarters in Minnesota. No way they could let them lose."

There's something about being down for so long that taints some people's views of the world, and they need a scapegoat to rationalize their disappointment. Again, I said that I had no doubt that the contest was legitimate.

"Then why did they post again when they weren't supposed to?"

I couldn't answer that one.

I wanted to call Cameron Potts to find out why there was an extra posting of the standings, but Karen wouldn't let me, at least not until I calmed down.

The next phone call was worse, because it had a ring of truth to it. Apparently, someone monitoring Facebook posts from Red Wing said that the night before, the public-address announcer at a Minnesota Wild National Hockey League Game had asked that everyone present vote for Red Wing. I had a vision of 15,000 Minnesota fans taking out their cell phones to vote, and my heart sank. That could have been what put them in the lead. Why didn't we think of that for the Sixers and Flyers?

I thought of the book I used to read my granddaughter, "Alexander and the Terrible, Horrible, No Good, Very Bad Day." That's the way things seemed to be going.

I wanted to do something constructive instead of wallowing in my pity. I shook it off and called John Cordisco, again! Talk about going to the well with someone! If anyone knew who ran the public-address system at the Wells Fargo Center in Philly, he would. I told him what happened. "John, we need someone at the Sixers or Flyers game to make a similar announcement."

John said he'd do his best. He had some angles to pursue. He called back a few minutes later with some bad news. "Both the Sixers and the Flyers are on road trips," he said.

My heart sank lower.

Then he added almost apologetically, "The circus is in town."

I felt my stomach knotting up. Somehow the circus just didn't sound as impressive, but I was desperate. "Well, can you get it announced there?"

"I knew you'd ask that, so I checked. The contacts I have would have been good for the Flyers or the Sixers, but it's an entirely different management company that controls events like the circus. Maybe you could work a different approach.

I hung up and called former Pennsylvania Lieutenant Governor, Jim Cawley. Jim was a very good friend of Bristol Borough and had offered his help. It was worth a shot. I've known Jim for over twenty years and have asked for scores of favors in the past. But asking him to get a public announcement made at the circus had to be the most unusual. Jim understood the importance and said he would go to work on it.

My daughter-in-law, Dana, came over with the kids, and I could tell she'd been crying over the Red Wing news. My daughter, Leighann, called from work and was just as upset. Both had worked extremely hard getting their respective faculties at School Lane Charter and Pennsbury on board, and I hated knowing they were distressed. I projected that to the hundreds of people who'd worked so hard.

Everyone who called had a different "I heard," story. Most were unsubstantiated nonsense. But still, I'd had enough. All of the rumors, innuendos and frustrations got the best of me, and I called Cam. It was obvious he was feeling the tension at his end of the line as well. He was probably getting bombarded by the other four towns for various reasons.

"Hey, Bill," Cam said. "I thought I'd hear from you."

"What's going on, Cam? Why was there an extra announcement contrary to what we were told would happen?"

Cam said they had thought about it a lot and when Red Wing moved into a slight lead, they decided it was only fair to let everyone know. He said we'd been leading all along, and they didn't want us to be shocked if we didn't win.

I would eventually feel that explanation was reasonable, but I wasn't feeling it in my current condition.

"Look, Cam, the way I see it, our guys have been killing themselves, doing all that they can. They just got an unexpected punch in the stomach. I'm afraid this will be a psychological letdown. And at the same time, Red Wing just got a tremendous and unexpected shot of energy, a big momentum boost."

Karen was watching me from the couch, giving me the eye not to overstep my place. We'd all become friends, and I knew she was right. Still, I was frustrated.

I could tell that Cam wasn't too pleased with me at that moment. He said that the race was extremely tight. "It's still anyone's race to win," he added.

I replied, "Cam, yesterday, you guys posted that more than 350,000 votes had been cast. It's probably up to 500,000 by now. As I see it, the tightening you're describing out of a half million cast is really a statistical tie.

I don't think he was looking for a suggestion, but I offered one anyway.

"You already did one additional update, maybe another is in order, one that says we're in a virtual tie, which I feel we are. It sounds a little less definitive than a 'new leader in the clubhouse.'"

Cam got quiet for a moment, then said. "I won't say it's a tie, because it's not, although it could change at any time. But the idea of another announcement seems fair to everyone. Let me talk to some people here and I'll get back to you."

He never did, but that afternoon SBR posted the following:

Due to the high volume of traffic as people rallied to vote for their towns, some of you may have experienced connection errors. We will be extending the vote window to MIDNIGHT eastern tomorrow. This will allow you to cast your votes tonight, and still be able to vote again tomorrow before the end of the competition. Please continue to refresh your browser until you are able to cast your vote.

I could only imagine how stressful things must have been for Cameron and the Deluxe team with people from all five towns battling down the home stretch.

Then the SBR team added this:

*It is a TIGHT race. **A dead heat at the top**, and very close throughout the rankings. It's still anyone's game. Thank you for your patience and good luck to all five towns!*

Bingo. A dead heat sounded a lot better than new leader in the clubhouse. It was a fair challenge to both towns to give it their best in the final hours. I shared it right away. Later, my son, Greg, told me he had a different take on what had transpired. He felt that Cameron was right to post the change when Red Wing took the lead, and that the post may have had the opposite effect to what I was thinking.

Knowing what happened next, I'd have to say he was right because **the people of Bristol didn't get discouraged as I feared they would. They got mad instead and channeled their anger into action.** The core team of Harry and Cathy Crohe, Shirley Brady,

Craig and Lynn Whitaker, Lorraine Cullen, Jim Sell, Joe Lelinski, Pat Mulhearn, Michael Crossan, Justin Saxton, Carl White, Bridget Shaw, Rosie Torres, my family, and so many more stepped up. The Grundy Library announced that they'd be open until midnight to allow access to their computer, so did the schools and the community college. People called their relatives from out of town to ask them to redouble their efforts. The outpouring was incredible and spontaneous, and it was beautiful to watch.

It stayed that way for the final twenty-four hours. At eleven PM on the final day, I posted the following: *One hour to go. I can't find the words to express how I feel about the absolutely wonderful people of Bristol Borough. Good, solid, proud, wonderful people. Karen and I love you all as much as you love our town. We all wish the other towns the best of luck. #mybristolborough*

I thought about a few lines from my favorite Teddy Roosevelt speech. The people of tiny Bristol Borough, people I grew up with, the children of people I grew up with, the people I see at WAWA every morning grabbing their coffee as they rush off to work. These people and their friends and family, near and far, truly **spent themselves in a worthy cause and had dared greatly.**

The winner wouldn't be announced for another week, but Deluxe had already done us an enormous favor that went beyond any financial reward or video exposure. They had challenged us to aspire to something big, and, in that regard, we had already won.

Chapter 22- Dancing Together

Well, in case you haven't picked up on it yet and the title didn't give it away, let me say again, WE WON. Later, on the night of the 22nd, Ralph and Monica DiGuiseppe stopped by the house. They suggested we should do something soon to bring the whole town together to celebrate. I added that we really should thank the entire county. We kicked around some ideas, including a parade, and settled upon a rally at the riverfront on Friday night, just two days later. The weather was predicted to be unseasonably warm and we decided to give it a shot. As it turned out, the Lord must have looked favorably on our effort because the temperature was a balmy 74 degrees.

It was a great night, and three days later I wrote the following guest editorial to the Bucks County Courier-Times. It's reprinted here because it captures the sense of thanks we felt that night.

We All Danced Together to Help Bristol Borough Win.

Bill Pezza

My wife, Karen, is big on thank-you cards. Send a gift or a kind gesture our way and you can be assured of a prompt response. That's why ever since Bristol Borough won the national Small Business Revolution contest on February 22, she has prefaced most of our conversations with the words, "Have you thanked...?" In most cases the answer has been, "Not yet, but I will." But how does one thank the thousands of people who helped, especially when so many did so anonymously? Thank God for print media. It's fitting that this message appears here, since the Bucks County Courier-Times/Intelligencer did so much to make our success possible. So, in behalf of the people of Bristol Borough, please accept our heartfelt thanks for a job done exceptionally well and for an inspiring outpouring of friendship from throughout the region.

Perhaps it would help to provide some context. It's been well documented on these pages that Bristol Borough had emerged as one of eight semifinalists out of 3500 towns nominated in a national Main Street Small Business Revolution contest. We had risen to that position solely through the nomination efforts of over one-hundred Bristol Borough residents- a laudable achievement in itself. Shortly thereafter, an exploratory visit by a team from Deluxe Corporation, the contest sponsors, resulted in our selection as one of five finalists. From there, the winner would be chosen by on-line national voting. It was at that point that Bristol Borough could not possibly make it on its own. With the hundreds of thousands of votes required to win, we would need an enormous effort by our own citizens, and the extensive assistance of good-willed people throughout the county and the entire Delaware Valley. Thankfully, we received both in levels beyond our most ambitious expectations. Now it's time to extend our thanks and congratulations to all who participated.

It's important to note that the people of Bristol Borough did not ask for help without first demonstrating with actions, not words, their strong commitment to help themselves. Their passion, their tireless effort, their enthusiasm, and their willingness to aspire to such heights was truly inspiring. While we will benefit greatly from Deluxe's $500,000 in small business marketing assistance, the intrinsic value of having achieved success while working hard together, of bonding in a way not seen in recent memory, of putting aside petty differences, was all the reward we needed, and the effort and lessons learned bode well for the future.

But, again, the herculean efforts of our people would not have been enough without the enthusiastic help of everyone who rallied to our cause: federal, state, county and local officials, major employers, educational institutions, fraternal organizations, celebrities, and others too numerous to mention, who were "all in."

With all of the attention the Borough received this month, there has been a very noticeable uptick in the number of visitors seen strolling on Mill Street, enjoying the architecture of Radcliffe Street or our cultural corridor, dining in our restaurants or taking in the construction of our boat docks on the Delaware River. No doubt the numbers will increase as the crews arrive to film the eight- part television documentary Deluxe will produce about Bristol Borough. The region is discovering us. But more importantly, we in the Borough have rediscovered ourselves.

Many old timers agree that the explosion of joy among the three hundred plus people in attendance at the Bristol Riverside Theater when the winning announcement was made was one of the greatest emotional moments in Bristol's proud history. I agree. But I was struck by what was for *me an equally emotional event that occurred two days later. It came during the Friday night town-wide celebration attended by over three thousand people. At one point, we sponsored a Bristol Stomp dance contest for little kids. There they were, ten or fifteen little boys and girls, none older than ten, black, white, Hispanic, smiling broadly as they danced their hearts out in front of so many happy on-lookers. I was struck by the fact that we've been dancing together in Bristol Borough since 1681, but rarely with this level of harmony. There's no limit to what we can do together if we keep the music playing.*

Thank you, Bucks County. Thank you, Delaware Valley. If you haven't already, find out why Bristol Borough is a wonderful place to visit, live or start a business.

Chapter 24- Courier-Times Editorial

Shane Fitzgerald is the executive editor of the Bucks County Courier-Times. Each Sunday he writes an opinion piece for the paper. It speaks volumes about the positive buzz Bristol Borough received in the county for the win.

Bucks County Courier-Times

'Gritty' Bristol Borough gets its due for its hard work

By Shane Fitzgerald, executive editor Feb 26, 2017
We all love a good underdog story. The kind where someone or something, against all odds, prevails in the end.
Bristol Borough won its Super Bowl on Wednesday.

Often described as "gritty" -- spend even an afternoon walking around downtown and you'll get that vibe -- the town of 9,500 was the last one standing among 14,000 nominations, 3,500 city/town entries and eight semifinalists to win the national Small Business Revolution contest.

The civic pride shown by Bristol Borough residents was amazing. Bill Pezza, chairman of the Raising the Bar civic association, was the driving force behind the initiative and rally that led Bristol to capture this $500,000 prize to help market the borough's small businesses. Last year's winner, Wabash, Indiana, has extolled the virtues of what this kind of exposure has done for its slice of Americana.

Pezza choked up when talking with reporters after finding out all the hard work, pride and effort had paid off so handsomely. As usual, Pezza deflected credit to those around him, but his force of will had more to do with this success than any single thing in the process.

It starts with the tone of the organization he leads -- Raising the Bar. That sends a message right there. It's a focus. It's a concept that people can rally around. Whether Pezza is teaching at Bucks County Community College or leading a charge like this, he is humble but driven to make a difference.

Bristol Borough has had the highest of highs and lowest of lows in its centuries-long existence. Bristol took a punch in the kisser when the mills closed a few decades ago and has been slowly building its way back up. This honor puts a little nitro in the fuel for this extraordinary town by the Delaware River.

Bristol didn't do this alone. Even if the borough's 9,500 residents each voted 100 times, that wouldn't have been enough to get the 1 million votes that ultimately were needed to earn this national recognition. So, it's clear its neighbors and friends rallied around the momentum the town had gained through the phases of the contest.

This is a great small-town story. Often, such civic pride rallies around a high school sports team, an annual festival or a unique quality a community possesses.

Bristol didn't have that easily identifiable characteristic. Although gritty has been thrown around to describe Bristol, grit isn't necessarily easily identifiable.

What this process showed is that despite all the lumps Bristol has taken over the years, its residents still have immense pride in their community. Pezza and several other borough leaders found a common cause. They had a vision, communicated it well and achieved something that not only will help Bristol, but also the surrounding communities on both sides of the river and down into Philadelphia.

Bristol's win is the region's win. The TV segments and publicity that follow this Small Business Revolution honor will keep the area top of mind beyond the euphoria Bristol's residents feel right now.

More than 200 people gathered in the Bristol Riverside Theatre and made a deafening roar when Amanda Brinkman, brand officer for contest sponsor Deluxe, stepped onto the stage to announce the winner. That moment undoubtedly will be etched in the minds of those in attendance. That kind of raw emotion and over-the-top happiness is something we don't get to see often. You can't help but want to cheer along.

Bristol Theatre board trustee Susan Atkinson said: "It's such a wonderful recognition of the passion of the town. I can't believe we won."

Of course, the next step is to make the most of this wonderful opportunity. The foot can't come off the gas pedal. Soon, next year's contest will begin and the pomp and circumstance will fade.

I have a feeling Bristol isn't going to let this pass by without taking advantage of it. I can't wait to see what's in store.

Congratulations, Bristol Borough. A job well done.

The most important comment in the piece is the next to last line, "I have a feeling Bristol isn't going to let this pass without taking advantage of it. I can't wait to see what's in store."

———————————

Neither can we!

Chapter 23- The Six

There were reports that the bars in towns had their best night in years following the announcement. Amanda Brinkman and Julie Gordon from Deluxe and Matt Naylor, the video's executive director from Flow/Non-Fiction; his producer, Tanya Belk; and cinematographer, David Layton, joined the crowd at the King George. The Philadelphia TV stations had interviewed several Borough residents following the afternoon theater announcement, and the interviews were now airing on the 6:00 news. Rick the Bartender worked the remote control to catch as many interviews as he could. It was much too loud to hear what was being said, but each time a borough resident's image appeared on the screen, the crowd in the packed tavern roared.

My phone vibrated, and it was Fox 29 News. They had filmed the announcement earlier, but their producers wanted an interview with me at 7:30 the following morning and wanted a crowd in the background. That was pretty short notice, but they had given us great coverage throughout the contest and I wanted to help them if I could.

I rang the ship's bell behind the bar to get the crowd's attention and announced that anyone who wanted to be on TV should meet at Mill Street Crossing at 7:15 the next morning. I said it would be fun, and I asked them to share the news on Facebook as well. There were spirited cheers, but I didn't expect much. I should have known better. The next morning there were two-hundred people at Mill Street Crossing when Fox 29 arrived, including parents with children on their way to school.

While the celebrating continued throughout the week, Deluxe got busy with the next phase of selecting the six businesses that would experience their intensive assistance and be featured in the video series.

Given the compact nature of the Borough, Deluxe determined that businesses throughout the town would be eligible to apply. They posted a link to the application and must have been floored by the response. Over one-hundred businesses applied, answering questions about their business, their goals, their struggles, their life stories.

Deluxe had made it clear from the outset that they weren't looking for the neediest businesses or the ones that were most successful. They were looking for businesses that would be the best fit for the services they offered, and whose owners had the most compelling story to share in the video series. They wanted the series to be instructive to small business viewers throughout the country, with each episode illustrating a valuable piece to the entrepreneurial experience. They also wanted a good cross section of business categories like restaurants, services, and retail. This wasn't to be another trite reality show where participants crashed and burned or were sent home or rejected. These were to be stories about real businesses growing, struggling, collaborating and finding success.

Next, they went about the private task of reviewing the applications to narrow the field to twenty. Speculation was rampant about whom should or would be picked. Many assumed I was privy to the deliberations because of my role in the contest. I explained that I had absolutely no role to play, nor did I want one. Some of the applicants were very good friends of mine. In fact, my son and daughter-in-law had applied for Itri, the restaurant/bar they were opening, as did several others who played a key role with Raising the Bar during the contest. Many asked me whether they should disqualify themselves from applying because of their position. My reply was the same for all. People in public life, or related to those who are, should be entitled to **no more** or **no less** consideration than anyone else. I advised that they just follow the guidelines and see where the process takes them.

Deluxe announced the twenty finalists and the list contained several surprises. The crew scheduled them for video interviews with Amanda Brinkman, Cameron Potts, Julie Gordon and Malcolm McRoberts, Deluxe's Senior Vice-president for small Business Services. They used the Centre for the Arts as their holding area where applicants would gather prior to their interview for make-up application and other preparations. The crew would also use the CFA for Amanda's wardrobe changes and to store their camera equipment between shooting sessions. Greg and Dana, who did not make the cut, donated their space at Itri, next door for the interview site.

For the next two days, the town watched though the large glass windows as the applicants took their spots across from the interview team, surrounded by cameramen, lighting and sound specialists. Itri looked like a film studio and the twenty finalists and their spouses were the actors.

The announcement of the winners surprised a lot of people, including, I think, the winners themselves. But the cross section of businesses, the stories they would tell, and the lessons they would convey through their interaction with the team from Deluxe, would turn out to be the perfect package for the video series that would feature them. They were about to be caught up in a whirlwind of remodeling, meeting with web designers and marketing experts, filming interviews, flying to Minnesota for more of the same, not to mention the surge in new business their new-found exposure would generate.

Below is an alphabetical listing of the businesses selected.

Annabella Restaurant, 119 Radcliffe Street. I have known owner Bobby Angelaccio forever and his wife Alison as a colleague at the community college for several years. Whether it was the result of Bobby's long-established family roots in Bristol Borough or the widely held opinion that he serves outstanding food, this was one of the most applauded choices of the "six." Described as "A taste of Italy nestled in Historic Bristol Borough," it is perfectly positioned across

107

from the Bristol Riverside Theater to attract theater goers for dinner prior to seeing a play.

Discover, Learn and Grow Early Learning Center is run by Romana Jones. It is located at the very top of Mill Street, across from our Mill Street Crossing site. On her webpage Ramona writes, "I've devoted my 30-year career to shaping young minds and nurturing the growth of children. We believe that each child is unique, and has an amazing capacity to discover, learn, and grow." The Center is active in the community and organized their parent base to assist with Bristol's most recent town-wide cleanup.

Hems Truck and Auto is located at the opposite side of town from Mill Street, at 2080 Farragut Avenue. It benefited from Deluxe's decision to expand eligibility town-wide. The Hems family has been involved in the borough business scene for over half a century. Co-owner Roland Hems' grandfather ran a trash hauling business, and his Uncle Fred ran a bookstore. Fred Hems is remembered by old timers as a tireless promoter of the borough. Long before social media and websites, Fred was known to distribute his "Boost Bristol" signs to whomever would have one.

Specializing in truck and auto repair, Roland Hems shares this quote on the company's website, "Working on cars is more than a job or a business — it's life, it's love, it's everything I think about, day and night."

Keystone Boxing and MMA Gym. Quoting from their new website, "Keystone Boxing & MMA Gym is dedicated to providing the youth and adults of the Bristol Borough area with a safe, positive and welcoming training environment. Our programs are designed to teach discipline, self-control and coordination while instilling confidence and commitment in members of all ages."

Keystone's proprietor, Jose Tilapa, is a ball of energy with an infectious, positive personality. He had played a big role during the week of voting prior to the February 22nd announcement. Not many people in town knew him, but those who did were happy for him. Since the contest, I've met people who send their very young children to the gym and are amazed by the growth of confidence and physical development they experience.

Miguel's Riverside Barbershop is located at 105 Market Street, just one block from the Bristol Riverside Theater and the Delaware River. It was necessary for the shop to be moved from its original location just around the corner on Radcliffe Street when the ownership of the building changed hands in the middle of the SBR makeover. The Riverside Barber Shop was established in 1923, and Miguel took over ownership in 2011. He is a popular figure in town and his new, fully remodeled location on Market Street bodes well for his future business.

Polka Dot Parlor is located at 324 Mill Street. Its website invites its customers to "Wear your fun, funky awesomeness on the outside. Polka Dot Parlor is all about looking good, feeling good and letting the real you come out to play." Polka Parlor's owner, Paulette Kasmer is a highly energized person who is expected to be a prominent voice for new business owners on Mill Street. I recommended her to Matt Naylor, to be my counterpart in the promotional video Deluxe and Flow/Non-Fiction prepared for the voting segment of the contest. He agreed, and she did an excellent job.

Chapter 25- The Big Shoot

Throughout the filming process, director Matt Naylor, in true artistic integrity, opted for spontaneous, authentic street scenes rather than staged ones. A necessary exception was what they called, "The big Shoots." These would be used as the opening segments to the series episodes. The plan was to have a crowd gathered at the base of Mill Street, with Amanda Brinkman, Robert Herjavec and the six featured business owners front and center as a drone camera took a wide view of Mill Street before zooming in on the stars and cheering supporters.

Raising the Bar's job was to publicize the event, invite the public to form the crowd, and make it known that street corner performers and vendors were welcome to add to the festive atmosphere. We posted the invitation on Facebook and notified the media. Craig Whitaker lined up street performers including Doo wop singers and children's characters.

Our pitch to the public was that they won the contest for Bristol with their voting, and they deserved to have some fun with this event. It ended up being a strong turnout, a great vibe for the town and another good day for the restaurants. After all, this is about small business development. The video crew did a few takes from different angles to get the drone shot just the way they wanted it. We won't know which shot made the final video or which of the candid street scenes would make the editor's cut until the series is released on the Hulu network and is streamed on the Small Business Revolution website, but for that shining moment, everyone on the street was a star.

When the scene shoot was over, Brinkman and Herjavec worked the crowd, with the film crew close behind. In probably the best spontaneous moment of the day, Herjavec did some finger snapping with the Doo Wop guys as they sang in front of the Mill Street Cantina, a scene that received thousands of "likes" on Facebook.

Prior to each visit from the film crew, Flow Non-Fiction's producer, Tanya Belk, would send me a filming schedule with a request to facilitate access to buildings and people scheduled to be interviewed. I love working with efficient people, and Tanya was the best. She planed her days to the minute, and it was fascinating watching the crew set up and breakdown as they moved from venue to venue. And the equipment they had was incredible, especially the drones and the 360-degree camera.

Chapter 26- Eyes on the prize

As I wrote earlier, this whole contest thing started with a post on Facebook showing Robert Herjavec's photo with the statement, "This man wants to give one small town in America $500,000, why not make it yours?" Shortly after we got involved a good friend of mine joked that he hoped Bristol didn't win because if we did some people would insist that I personally got the $500,000. Such is the nature of small towns.

Well, Bristol won, and, as suspected, Karen and I DID get the $500,000 deposited directly to our account. We took a month-long cruise in the Caribbean, put a down payment on a nice little place at the shore, and banked the rest for the grandkids. **I'm kidding, of course.**

At every step of the contest it was clear that Deluxe controlled the purse strings. No money would be released to the Borough or any individuals. Contractors and venders would be paid directly by Deluxe as vouchers were submitted for their work. Furthermore, much of the prize would come in the form of in-kind technical assistance from experts in retail, accounting, marketing, branding, web design, remodeling, inventory tracking, shipping and more.

In the interest of full disclosure, I did receive two books from Deluxe in recognition of my work with them. Cameron Potts had told Ron McGuckin that they wanted to give me a small personal gift to present at the closing ceremony and were looking for suggestions. Ron told them I collected biographies of presidents, so they presented me with a biography of George Bush 41 and Barack Obama. Both are proudly displayed on my book shelf and serve as a lasting memory of the friendships with Deluxe built throughout the contest.

I'll digress for a moment to add that while I have biographies of thirty-six presidents in my collection, I'm still missing Zachary Taylor,

Millard Fillmore, James Buchanan, Benjamin Harrison, Warren G. Harding, Herbert Hoover, Gerald Ford, and the current occupant, whose name escapes me. These are not exactly household names, and it's been a struggle to find them. If your ever come across one…

Anyway, back to the real prizes. Winning the Small Business Revolution-Main Street contest yielded a generous amount of tangible and intangible rewards both for the Borough as a whole and its individual businesses. For me, it's the intangibles that matter most. Winning gave our town a tremendous shot of energy, confidence, optimism and unity that should pay dividends long after the hype surrounding the contest fades. **It has dramatically changed how we see ourselves and how others see us.** I'm optimistic about where we're going, but this is really one of those carpe diem moments. Will the organization and culture of success we've put in place seize the day and implement the call for action found in the last section of this book? I think it will, but we'll see. For now, let's examine the tangible rewards we received from the contest.

The Video

From the moment the Deluxe team came to town in January 2017 until the final video crew left in August, everything that had taken place was captured in hundreds of hours of film, and, at the time of this writing, the skilled team of film editors and writers from Flow/Non-Fiction are converting that raw footage into eight documentary episodes, totaling four hours, about the resurgence of business and community spirt in Historic Bristol Borough. Having watched the full SBR Season 1 documentary about Wabash, Indiana, there's no doubt the Season 2 series will be a home run for us. Make that a grand slam, especially since it will be released nationally on the Hulu network as well as streamed on the SBR website. **This will be a priceless marketing tool moving forward.**

Commercial District Improvements

Cameron Potts asked me to compile a proposed list of projects the Borough and Raising the Bar would like as part of Deluxe's gift to the Borough. The criterion was that the gifts were to stimulate business or tourism, and the final decision would rest with Deluxe. Our list included a pavilion at the upper end of Mill Street for use as a weekend farmers market, a quality sound system for Riverfront Park, sets of sidewalk poles to support banners announcing upcoming festivals and other events, a kiosk to hold a walking map of the commercial district and Cultural Corridor. The projects we proposed needed to be completed by early July, in time to be filmed for the final episodes.

As it turned out, the construction schedule required for the pavilion was too extended, and we had to scrap the idea. Deluxe did implement the remaining projects, highlighted by a state-of-the-art sound system that extends the length of the Riverfront Park, including the pier, and the 100 block of Mill Street. The system will be a valued enhancement to our Christmas tree lighting ceremony, which we believe is the best in Bucks; the Lion's Sunday evening summer concerts, our ethnic festivals, First Fridays and other special events and ceremonies like the Elk's Flag Day observance.

It the absence of events, the Borough also plans to play soft music in the park all day and early evening for visitors to enjoy.

Website Design

Deluxe has a first-class marketing team whose talented web department designs pages high on both style and substance. In what could prove to be the gift with the most impact on economic growth, they designed a site that we're calling "Visit Bristol." Its focus will be dining, the arts, shopping and nightlife. It will also showcase our natural resources like the riverfront, the marsh, the canal, and historic district, and will publicize festivals and other special events. It will provide links to our major restaurants, the Bristol Riverside Theater, the Centre for the Arts, the Grundy Museum and Library, the Historic Society, the Bristol Borough Business Association and Visit Bucks.

Of course, once a website is established, the real work is keeping it current. Raising the Bar has retained a web manager for this purpose. Updates will flow through our organization to him. This includes new photos to keep the site fresh and seasonally correct. Julie Gordon was the Deluxe point person for this project and did an excellent job. The web address is www.visitbristolborough.com and went live in mid-September.

Marketing Seminar

Deluxe flew in a team of experts from Minnesota to conduct a free seminar on using webpages and social media as marketing tools. The event was held at the Bristol Riverside Theater and over 100 current or aspiring business owners attended. They also conducted a business discussion for aspiring entrepreneurs at the Bristol campus of Bucks County Community College and Bristol High School. Jim Sell and Tracy Timby facilitated the college event and Heather Quattrocchi coordinated the high school visit. Raising the Bar's Economic Development subcommittee, headed by Don McCloskey and Jim Sell, is working on providing an ongoing series of seminars to assist small business owners in the Borough to sustain what Deluxe has started.

Working with the Six

Beyond all of this, the bulk of Deluxe's work was focused on the six businesses in the video series. All received capital improvements either in the form of facade upgrades, signage or interior

115

enhancements.

From the outset, Deluxe wanted to use Borough contractors for the work. RTB board member, Justin Saxton of Construction Building Materials, provided Deluxe with a comprehensive list of contractors and their contact information. It was the height of the construction season, and we were surprised to learn that many contractors were already committed to other jobs. Some were able to defer that work to complete the Deluxe projects within the film schedule parameters.

Coordinating all of this with a sponsor based in Minnesota wasn't easy. This was especially true when it came to assistance about design, color selections, and lining up vendors for furnishings and equipment. RTB board member, Mycle Gorman owns Design works on Mill Street. He donated his time and expertise to assist Deluxe and the six business owners with the design process, and did a remarkable job. **I like to call Mycle the unofficial Mayor of Mill Street because of his commitment to the success of the commercial district. He gives freely of his time, talent and treasure to the cause.**

Each of the six businesses received a new web page. They also received assistance with branding and "Telling their story." Finally, they were all flown to Minnesota at Deluxe's expense for three days of intensive workshops and discussions with Robert Herjavec, Amanda Brinkman and other experts.

Seed Money

The last piece of the prize came in the form of a $10,000 grant to Raising the Bar to continue the work we've been doing to advance business and tourism in the Borough.

That's what Deluxe did for us. It remains to be seen what we will do for ourselves moving forward.

Part III

Seed Planters

"One Generation plants the seeds, and another enjoys the shade."
Chinese proverb.

The primary focus of this book has been to celebrate Bristol's recent accomplishments, and to use them as a call to action to join the Raising the Bar and Borough Council efforts to keep the momentum going. But while our town's success seems be to growing at an exponential rate, it might be easy to forget or never really take the time to appreciate the tremendous work done by individuals and organizations who came before us.

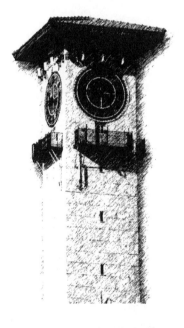

In some of the most difficult times of the past, when spirits were not as high and confidence not as widespread, there were still those who kept the dream alive, who doggedly held on to a vision and worked to make it a reality. In doing so, they laid the groundwork for much of what we enjoy today. Part III is dedicated to them. It is by no means intended to be all inclusive, and again, I apologize in advance for omissions. It is rather an attempt in the time and space available to shine a bright light on the accomplishments of some remarkable individuals and organizations. Some are "bricks and mortar" stories, while others are more intangible or symbolic, but all, I believe, offer inspiring examples of what civic minded people can accomplish, even in difficult times.

As the quote above reads: *One generation plants the seeds, and another enjoys the shade.* What follows are a few brief stories about some exceptional seed planters.

Chapter 27- Leonard Snyder: From X to BRT. Picking us up after we bottomed out.

I have fond childhood memories of walking to the Bristol movie theater with my friends to catch a Saturday matinee. Admission was twenty-five cents and popcorn cost a dime. One of my favorite films was the Walt Disney production of Tonka, a story about a wild stallion, a young Indian brave, and Custer's last stand. It was thrilling. The theater remained a quaint part of the Borough until...

It's difficult to pinpoint when any town in decline hits rock bottom. Surly the slide begins when a major employer shuts down or drastically reduces staff. It becomes more apparent when shops begin to fall victim to malls and big box stores. But when does a town actually hit bottom? It's usually hard to tell. But for Bristol Borough, I can pin-point the exact event. It was when the Bristol movie theater could no longer compete with the newer theaters opening in the area and closed its doors just long enough to convert to an X- rated movie house! Virtually overnight Bristol Borough was stigmatized by hosting the only X-rated theater in the area. It reaffirmed the low regard many in the country already held for the Borough. Just like the Nathanial Hawthorn character, Hester Prynn, was forced to wear a scarlet A on her clothing to identify her as an adulterer, Bristol was seemingly marked with a big red x in the minds of Bucks County residents.

To make matters worse, the theater was located in the heart of our commercial district, on the first block of Historic Radcliffe Street. It stood out like an angry pimple on the town's nose. Residents were mortified and legally helpless to do anything since the changeover preceded newer zoning ordinances that could have regulated the use. Seeing the marque advertising films like "Debbie Does Dallas" or "Deep Throat" was like getting a pin prick to the eyeball. In fact, any mention of Dallas in the Philadelphia Eagles territory is like a pin

119

prick to the eyeball, but that's another story. Back to the theater.

A good friend recently confessed to me that she and her brother threw eggs at the X-rated movie house in defiance. I told her the statute of limitations had expired if she allowed me to use her name here, but she declined. Anyway, her actions were representative of the frustration shared by many.

Fortunately, help was on the way in the form of the Grundy Foundation's Executive Director, Leonard Snyder, and its Board of Directors. In one of the most visionary and dramatic moves in Bristol's modern history, the Foundation purchased the building and was instrumental in its transformation into an award winning performing arts theater. Kudos also to Susan Atkinson who lobbied hard for idea and highly talented people like **Keith Baker, Susan Atkinson, and Anne Kohn** who carry the standard of excellence today. The Bristol Riverside theater celebrated its 30th Anniversary in 2017. Today it attracts over 40,000 ticket holders per year, a majority from out of town. These visitors fill our restaurants, tour our commercial district and become ambassadors for Bristol, sharing their positive experience with others when they return home. It is one of our strongest cultural and economic development assets. That big red x has turned into a proud and glowing BRT!

For newcomers to town or those too young to remember a darker time, it's important for everyone to know the debt of gratitude we owe to the Grundy Foundation for the decisive action it took more than thirty years ago. Just as it is difficult to pinpoint when a town bottoms out, it is difficult to identify a specific event that puts it on the road to recovery. But there is no doubt that the Foundation's acquisition and subsequent decision to convert the building to a performing arts facility ranks near, if not at, the top.

Bravo!

Chapter 28- Paul Ferguson and Bucket of Paint

W. Paul Ferguson was a man ahead of his time. In an era when less value was placed upon the preservation of our historic architecture and natural resources, Paul was a champion of both. He served as chairman of the Borough's Historic and Architectural Review Board (HARB), an entity charged with ensuring that building renovations in our historic district conform to preservationist standards. This notion was not always popular with those who felt it flew in the face of an individual's freedom to do what he pleased with his property. But the courts have been clear that government has the power to regulate private property in the public interest, provided such regulation is reasonable. Of course, property owners and preservationists often have differing views on what is reasonable. But Paul was steadfast in enforcing the code because he understood that once a building's façade loses its architectural integrity, it is most likely gone forever. Paul wasn't alone in this belief, but he was certainly in a distinct minority. Fortunately, a growing number of people in town have "caught up" with Paul's thinking, and people like Donna McCloskey, the Executive Director of the Grundy Museum, and RTB Board member Robin Butrey, as well as current HARB members and others are carrying the torch.

Paul was also an early member of the Delaware-Lehigh Navigation Canal National Heritage Corridor Commission. That's certainly a mouthful, but don't blame me; I didn't name the group. Anyway, the Commission's purpose was to preserve, enhance and market the canal as a national treasure. Paul became a strong presence on the commission, arguing strenuously for more emphasis to be placed on the previously neglected "lower end" of the canal. Fortunately, this advocacy is carried today by activists like Susan Taylor of the Friends of the Delaware Canal, Elissa Garofalo of the D & L and Ron McGuckin of Raising the Bar.

Paul was a throwback to an earlier era in manner and speech. He spoke in a measured, deliberate cadence and smoked a pipe long after the practice had been abandoned by almost everyone. He even occasionally wore a tweed jacket with leather reinforced elbows. He was a gentleman by any standard, but he could be prickly when it came to his values, and he wasn't afraid to roll up his sleeves for the right cause.

Paul passed in 2003, and will be remembered for his many contributions to the Borough. However, **it was his resolve in a confrontation with an unseen adversary that captured my attention and should serve as a valuable lesson for all of us.**

Bristol's Old Quaker Cemetery on Wood Street is a cherished spot in the Borough. Local historian, Harold Mitchener told me that the cemetery dates back to the very early 1700s. it is truly beautiful in its simplicity.   There is a long wall that separates the cemetery from the sidewalk along Wood Street. The wall is a three-foot high white stucco structure topped with a black wrought-iron fence that rises another two feet. It makes for a charming border for the hallowed ground it encloses. At some point a vandal decided to spray paint symbols and messages on the white surface, and it looked hideous. This was years before organizations like Towns Against Graffiti were formed and funded to remove graffiti promptly and effectively. Most defacing of public places usually remained untouched, especially on old, abandoned buildings or structures belonging to groups or individuals with limited resources to remove it.

Many of us would ride by the marred wall and shake our heads in disappointment and complain about the defacing that had taken place, but Paul did more than shake his head. Armed with a couple of gallons of paint and a roller, Paul simply repainted the wall. Soon after, as anticipated, the vandal was back and the wall was defaced again. So, Paul returned with more paint and covered the graffiti **again!** This went on for three cycles until the unknown vandal gave up. I'm convinced Paul would have gone on for ten rounds or even twenty if that was what it would take to make his point.

Paul Ferguson saw something that didn't rise to the standards he held for his town, and he did something about it. He didn't wait for someone else to take care of it; he took action. This might be one small story in the scheme of things, but if we all followed Paul's lead, well, simply stated, things would be better.

I love Chinese proverbs, and Paul's actions illustrated one of the better known but less followed. "It is better to light a single candle than to curse the darkness."

Bravo, Paul. Well done.

Chapter 29- Corrigan, Tomlinson, A Canal, and A Vision

Each spring in Bristol Borough visitors gather at the beautiful Canal Lagoon Park on Jefferson Avenue to launch their kayaks, paddleboards, canoes, or rowboats and join in a floating parade. Spectators bring their lawn chairs and enjoy live music, good food and games and prizes for the kids. It is a fun family event in a wonderfully preserved natural setting of historical significance. If the visitors took the time to examine the kiosk that overlooks the lagoon, they would gain insight into one of the greatest conservation projects led by volunteers in Pennsylvania history. It took place in 1997 and was spearheaded by **State Representative Tom Corrigan, State Senator Tommy Tomlinson, AFL-CIO President Mike Peterpaul, and North Ward Councilman, Joe Coffman.**

The original Delaware-Lehigh Navigation Canal spanned eastern Pennsylvania from the White Haven-Jim Thorp area in the north to its southern terminus in Bristol Borough. Today, it represents a vital part of our nation's transportation and commercial history. In 1940 the Pennsylvania legislature designated the canal, towpath and adjacent areas as a state park, and in 1988, the United States Congress created the Delaware & Leigh National Heritage Corridor.

Bristol Borough is a vital part of the Heritage Corridor story because it was in Bristol that the canal met the Delaware River. One can still see the ring foundation that once supported the crane that would off-load cargo from the barges and canal boats on to vessels at the Delaware River that would carry the coal, wheat and other commodities to Philadelphia and beyond. One can imagine the flurry of commercial activity at the site during the peak of the canal era.

Less than a mile from the ring is the aforementioned canal lagoon. The lagoon is significantly wider than the canal bed because it was once the spot used as the holding area for boats and barges waiting to take their turn at the crane. It was also a place for canal boats heading to the river to "pull over" so to speak, so barges headed back north to the coal region could pass.

By the 1990s the area had fallen into serious disrepair. It had become the site of an ice skating rink that had caught fire and was eventually torn down. The lagoon's retaining walls were crumbling and the clay liner had deteriorated to the point where it was difficult to keep water in the lagoon. What little water did remain was virtually stagnant and overwhelmed by algae. The lagoon area had "bottomed out" in a literal sense.

What happened next was one of the most inspiring and effective partnerships between government, labor and the private sector that I have seen in over forty years of public life. I wrote about it in a commemorative booklet printed in 1997, and excerpts are recounted here.

State Representative Tom Corrigan and Senator Tommy Tomlinson secured a modest grant to improve the area, but they knew it wouldn't be enough. They met one night with Mike Peterpaul, President of the Bucks County AFL-CIO. The meeting took place at the Ancient Order of Hibernians on Corson Street. They told Mike about the funding they received and wondered if they could "stretch" the grant a little by using volunteers for some of the labor.

Peterpaul was receptive and the idea began to grow. Why not make the Bristol Lagoon a showplace for the entire Delaware Canal by seeking voluntary participation from business and labor? Soon Waste management, Inc. had agreed to become a partner, and Corrigan, Tomlinson and Peterpaul had secured the help of seven different trade unions. Led by Peterpaul, Bruce Jones of the Operating Engineers Local 542, Harry McGuckin of the Carpenter's Local 1462, Jim Giglio of the Cement Masons Local 592 and Tom Bates of IBEW Local 269, over one hundred and seventy union volunteers donated what amounted to thousands of hours of labor to the project. They were joined by almost forty private volunteers from the Borough. Corrigan became the hands-on project manager and was assisted by Councilman **Joe Coffman**. Operating engineer **John Scholl** did exceptionally skillful work in excavating and lining the bed with clay donated by Waste management.

I found an old quote from **Harry McGuckin** at the time. He said, "People ask me why I did the project. I did it because Tommy Corrigan and Tommy Tomlinson asked me to. That's why." And that about sums it up. Those guys had a force of will that was difficult to say no to.

From the private sector, fifty-six corporations, businesses, service organizations and social clubs joined Waste Management in donating materials, services and equipment to the project. The modest plan to "dress up" the area had grown to a first class environmental and historical restoration project valued conservatively in excess of three million dollars of in-kind contributions.

There was a "can do" attitude throughout the project. I remember at one point, a canal advocate from one of the northern towns said smugly while the work was in progress, "You'll never get water in the lagoon." The person had a point. It had become increasingly difficult to keep water flowing south from the upper reaches of the canal and the bed would often be dry. But that person didn't know Tom Corrigan very well. He brought in a contractor and drilled a well. Today, even during the longest droughts, the lagoon is NEVER without water!

At the time of the project, I was the legislative assistant to Tom Corrigan, and **Jim Cawley** was my counterpart for Senator Tomlinson. Corrigan and I were democrats and Tomlinson and Cawley were republicans. Jim and I would often discuss how great it was that our bosses worked hand in hand to get things done for their constituents without concern for partisan politics.

I remember one Sunday morning when Corrigan called during the project with a bit of a crisis. The contractor who had donated the metal forms for the pouring of the concrete retaining walls needed them by Monday morning for another project. The walls were finished and the concrete had set, but the forms were still attached and needed to be separated. The metal pins had to be removed so the contractor could quickly remove the forms the following morning. Tom was looking for help wherever he could get it.

For the rest of the day, Jim Cawley and I stood side by side in three inches of clay mud removing the pins. Jim would later go on to become Lieutenant Governor of the Commonwealth of Pennsylvania and I...well, I'm just doing my thing.

Occasionally, I'll see a wedding party or prom kids having their pictures taken at the restored gazebo on the island in the middle of the beautifully watered lagoon and my thoughts turn to Corrigan, Tomlinson, Peterpaul and McGuckin, and the hundreds of volunteers who worked there and the scores of businesses that donated. I hope the people who enjoy the lagoon today remember them as well.

There is a quote by Corrigan on the kiosk at the lagoon that reads, "Everyone we asked for help said yes." That's a good model of citizen involvement to follow as we move forward in Bristol Borough.

Chapter 30- Don McCloskey

I was Borough Council President when Don arrived on the Council in 1985. It didn't take long to realize that Don would be a bright, hard-working, progressive member of council. We were soulmates, so to speak, sharing a vision and a sense of urgency to get things done. It was a time of block grants and funding sources for a myriad of programs. We worked together to replace the dangerous and environmentally harmful rail spur line through town and allow for the property expansion of the Bristol Riverside Theater. Don sold me on the idea of installing brick sidewalks, antique lighting and planting trees on Mill Street. When he doggedly convinced a majority of business owners to vote to assume matching financial responsibility for the project, I knew he would be an effective voice for Bristol Borough. What I didn't know is that he would go on to serve for twenty-years, most as council president, and would usher in a long series of improvements and build strong public/private partnerships.

Knowing that progress comes incrementally and is often evaluated within the context of its time, I believe the improvements during his tenure physically and psychologically set the stage for the ongoing revitalization of the town.

The examples below are just some of the improvements made by him, his fellow council members and borough professional colleagues like solicitor **Rich Snyder** during their time in office that we may take for granted today.

- Acquisition/demolition and redevelopment of Riverfront North – eliminating most industrial presence and increasing residential use along the river.
- Acquisition and rerouting of the rail spur through the center of town

- Creation of Spurline park on the footprint of the former rail line that connects other walking areas in town resulting in approximately 4-mile walking, jogging area.
- Creation of the conservation easement on both sides of the Bristol Marsh protecting the marsh in perpetuity and allowing active and passive recreation
- The revitalization of the public space on Mill Street through a special assessment of owners
- Density reduction program of acquisition/demolition of high density residential buildings
- Aggressive program of density reduction through property acquisition of rehabilitation to a lesser number of units per building.
- Sale of the municipal water system and creation of a cash reserve of $26M – still in place.
- Construction of the municipal ice skating complex
- Creation of gateways into the borough
- Enhancement and reconstruction of the borough waterfront with the creation of a new pier and park directly behind the Bristol Riverside Theatre.
- Facilitated the land use changes to enable the construction of the Bristol Riverside Theatre.
- Transferred borough land to the school district and funded the creation of the track and practice fields adjacent to the school
- Created/upgraded municipal playgrounds throughout the town
- Upgraded the existing playing fields and created new soccer fields across town
- Four sections of town were formally research and assigned status in the National Register of Historic Places.

Recently, I was able to recruit Don out of retirement to chair the Economic Development Sub-Committee of Raising the Bar.

Currently their primary focus is to provide seminars and programs to assist new and existing businesses. We're happy to have him in the game again, but grateful for the exceptional stewardship he displayed during his previous tenure.

31- Historic Bristol Day

If George Washington slept in half the places that towns up and down the eastern seaboard claim he did, then it's a wonder that we won the revolution or got anything accomplished in the early days of our republic. There are no Rip Van Winkle references to how long he slept in each place or whether there was an early American equivalent of Expedia or Travelocity to help him find lodging, but he certainly got around, and historical societies from New Hampshire to the Carolinas won't let you forget it. The point is that people love history, and towns that recognize this by cultivating their stories and preserving relics and period architecture do themselves a service.

Bristol Borough is loaded with history and is fortunate to have had individuals and groups who have worked to document, share and preserve it.

The Radcliffe Cultural and Historical Foundation was founded by well- known Bristol Artist, Joe Pavone. As the name suggests, the group was formed to promote the history and culture of the Borough. I still have my charter membership card somewhere. I wasn't a very active member, devoting my time instead to my duties as a Borough Councilman, but I paid my dues and cheered them on as they advanced their goals. Eventually the name was changed to the Bristol Cultural and Historical Foundation to broaden their scope.

In October of 1977, Foundation members Mary Jane Mannherz and Pauline White conceived of and implemented the first Historic Bristol Day. Mannherz, who directed the Grundy Library for decades until her retirement a few years ago, recently wrote, "Historic Bristol Day was conceived as a celebration to highlight the early eighteenth century roots of Bristol Borough, and thereby to instill community pride and recognition of our town's place within the history of our nation. The first Historic Bristol Day, October 15, 1977, featured a Revolutionary War encampment at the Bristol Wharf and their march down Radcliffe Street; reenactors at Bristol's 18th century buildings who explained their 1780's life, and demonstrations of home industries including: soap making, candle making, blacksmithing, cooking, tinsmithing and more."

Bingo! I remember it well, and it was a smashing success. Mary Jane, Pauline, and their committee, put considerable effort into the planning, and they continued the program for two more years before passing it off to others. The day has grown to be one of the fall highlights in Lower Bucks County, a truly feel good, family day that attracts visitors throughout the county, but it was the vision, leadership, and attention to detail by Mary Jane and Pauline that got it going. Since then, dedicated volunteers like Anna Larrisey, Patricia Stallone, Harold and Carol Mitchener, Mary Gesualdi, Helen Younglove, Robin Butrey, Donna McCloskey, Louise Davis, Anne Walp, Jan Ruano and many others perpetuate this wonderful tradition in the Borough.

Joe Pavone is no longer with us, and Mary Jane and Pauline have retired, but no doubt all three take pleasure in knowing that the organization and event they started remains one of the highlights of Bristol Borough's calendar year. Bravo to them all.

Chapter 32- A "Pride" of Lions

Each year in late summer, thousands flock to the riverfront in Bristol Borough to enjoy the Italian Day festival, the largest of the wonderful ethnic gatherings that celebrate the Borough's diversity. They feast on sausage, meatball, or veal and pepper sandwiches, pizza, water ice and baked goods like pizzelles or biscotti. Later in the evening they enjoy the live music that emanates from the gazebo in the park. In fact, there is an outdoor concert every Sunday night from May until September. People bring their lawn chairs and boaters anchor at the river's edge to listen. It is a totally enjoyable way to spend a summer evening and is one of the Borough's finest traditions. In fact, the riverfront festivals and concerts are constantly showcased on websites, Facebook pages and visitor brochures as one of Bristol's prime attractions.

We can enjoy the festival, the concert gazebo, and many of the improvements at the park today because of the vision, dedication and generosity of a group of men who made up the core of the Bristol Lions club in the early 1970s, men like Tony Zanni, Angelo Quattrocchi, Tony Boccardo, Angelo Liccardello, Tony Mandio, Al Magro, Frank Mignoni, Henry Perotti, Roy Butterworth, Joe Stallone, and others. It was they who launched the first Italian Day Festival more than thirty years ago. It was they who envisioned, designed, financed and constructed the gazebo in the mid-1970s. And it was they who enhanced the landscaping and other amenities in the park. Furthermore, their actions became the stimulus for the development of other ethnic celebrations like Celtic Day, Puerto Rican Day, and African-American Day.

Lions travel in prides in their natural habitat, and I thought it would be an appropriate play on words to describe these men who I looked up to in my younger days as an elected official. Each was successful in his own right as business leaders in town, but they found the time to serve their community selflessly and with foresight. Another thing that struck me about them is that they clearly took pride in their work and enjoyed the camaraderie and satisfaction that working together for a common purpose can bring.

Many have since passed away, but their legacy of service lives on as the current Lions Club members continue their work, men like Ron Walker, Angelo Grisolia, Joe Fida, Bob Kaufman, and the newest Lions President, Mycle Gorman.

Community leaders, whether they are elected officials, business leaders, service club members or Raising the Bar volunteers, have a responsibility of stewardship, which Webster defines as **the careful and responsible management of something entrusted to one's care.** We have all been entrusted with the care and advancement of our town, to leave it in better condition than we found it.

The "pride" of lions mentioned above certainly left the Bristol Borough Riverfront in much better condition than they found it. I think if they were here today they wouldn't ask for gratitude, although they surely deserve it. They would ask that each of us find a form of service to our town that we enjoy and leave a legacy as they did.

Chapter 33- "It's Good to Shop on Friendly Mill Street ..."

As a young man, I remember some of the old timers who led the business association during the street's heyday and struggled to hang on as the malls emerged to compete. Men like the Profy brothers, Leon Plavin, Frank Mignoni, Carmen and Carolyn Mignoni, Charlie Richmond, Leon Kanter, Rob Normal, Sid Popkin, Ed Bundy, and others were hustlers who worked hard to keep the street vibrant. Many made their homes above their stores and took great pride in the appearance of their properties. They were community minded and participated in various civic groups.

They knew how to draw a crowd. They sold appliances, tires, shoes, clothing, jewelry, bicycles, records, toys, and just about anything a consumer would want. They coined the jingle, "It's good to shop on friendly Mill Street in Bristol, Pa." and ran it, along with its recognizable lead in musical notes, constantly on WBCB radio. Some, like Leon Plavin, were exceptionally passionate about the town and their businesses, and could become rather excitable. At times, they'd clash with Borough Council over services or police protection. Others, like Vince Profy, were calming influences. All were totally hands on, tireless workers.

Their advancement in age coincided with the decline of main streets across America and it was somewhat sad to see them close or sell their stores as they prepared for retirement or move them to another location for the next generation in the family to carry on. I thought about them recently when I was doing a photo shoot of new construction on the street. There were dumpsters and ladders seemingly everywhere as property owners gutted their buildings in preparation for new business openings or implemented their DCED façade grants to renovate the front of their buildings. It was exciting to see all of the action.

I wondered what they would think of the newest generation of entrepreneurs. People like Tim McGinty of the Mill Street Cantina, Joe Rakowski of Nobel Earth, Greg and Dana Pezza of itri wood fired pizza bar, J.P. Lutz of Bucks County Baseball, Andrew & Jodi Dittman of Calm Waters, Paulette Kasmer of Polka Dot Parlor boutique, Jimmy Bason of Bird of Paradise Flowers, Matthew and Michele Howard of Healthy Plates, and the proprietors of the plethora of new beauty salons and men's grooming shops on the street.

I think they would view the shift in emphasis to restaurants and specialty shops as an adaptation to the new economic realities, and they would approve. I think the old timers, more than anyone, would appreciate the grit, determination, sweat and worry that accompanies new business ownership and I think they'd be cheering for their old street where they had invested decades of their lives. They were economic pioneers, and we should not forget them.

Chapter 34- Harold and Carol Mitchener

Harold and his wife Carol have spent a lifetime researching, documenting and lecturing about the history of Bristol's buildings, commercial past, notable residents and events. Speaking with them about Bristol Borough is like having a conversation with a human search engine. Their knowledge is broad, deep and available with instant recall. In a contest between the Mitcheners and Google about Bristol's History, I'd bet heavily on the Mitcheners. Give them a street address and they will rattle off information about the architecture, builder, and notable past inhabitants. You'll hear about old sea captains, relatives of former presidents, homes that were won or lost in card games. It's fun.

In 2000 Arcadia published the Mitcheners' book, *Bristol, Pennsylvania*, as part of the Images of America series. It is a wonderful collection of photos and narratives of Historic Bristol Borough from its founding in 1681 to the near present. It is a treasure of information that every Bristol resident and fan should have. Among Bristol's treasures are the Mitcheners themselves, not only for following their calling to study history, but for sharing their knowledge so freely and skillfully. For years they have served as tour guides, portrayed historic figures in dramatizations, and volunteered for countless hours in community projects. Their work has been cited repeatedly in newspaper articles, pamphlets and commemorative booklets.

In recent years, they have wisely decided to archive their materials and information, as well as the information of others at the Grundy Library. Working closely with the library's director, **Dana Barber**, the Grundy Museum's director, Donna McCloskey, and with assistance from the Grundy Foundation, they are preserving resources that will be utilized for many years to come.

One can only hope that others will emerge to become the next generation of historians to study, share and preserve the rich history of Bristol Borough.

Quiet Heroes

There are so many others, both from the public and private sector, who've worked selflessly for the town for years, and whose unassuming manner keep them in the background.

They would warrant a chapter of their own if time and space permitted a full recounting of their generous contribution of time, talent or treasure over an extended period. But at the very least, they deserve our thanks and recognition here for going well above and beyond. Again, I do this at the risk of overlooking others and apologize in advance for omissions.

Ron Walker

Jim Dillon

Bill Salerno

Merle Winslow

Gene Williams

Louis Quattrocchi

JoAnna Schneyder

Carol Ferguson

John Mundy

Joe Larrisey

Donnie Petolillo

Herb Slack

Part IV

Game Changers

We all serve in our own ways, and some make such a contribution that they change the physical or psychological landscape of the town. They may bring about a significant shift in how we do things, our approach to problems, our vision of what can be done next. Their contributions and efforts inspire us to raise the bar of expectations we hold for ourselves and how we may empower others. We call them **Game Changers**, and Part IV profiles some of the most prominent.

Chapter 35- Ralph DiGuiseppe

I've known Ralph DiGuiseppe forever. Back in 1979 his mother, Rose, helped me get elected to Borough Council for the first time. Later, Rose got elected in her own right, and we served together for a few years. Fast forward twenty years and Ralph had become one of the better-known builders in town. Karen and I had just bought an old home and needed someone to build an addition and completely redo the kitchen and bathrooms. I thought of Ralph. He had just built a new home for Helen Younglove on Mansion Street, and he suggested I speak with her about the quality of his work. I did, and she was effusive in her praise. We contracted with Ralph, and he did a terrific job. Some builders build and leave, but Ralph made it clear that he wasn't going anywhere until we were completely satisfied. We were. I think you can learn a lot about how a person's approach to his livelihood carries over to is approach to government and his attention to detail.

During the construction, Ralph was preparing to follow in his mother's footsteps by running for Borough Council himself. He knew I did a lot of campaign literature work and asked if I would help him with his first piece. I agreed and we met in his kitchen to go over what he wanted to include. Ralph was excited and had a ton of ideas. We started with a draft flyer, which soon changed to a two-sided handout. Then it became a four-page brochure. Ralph just kept adding things he wanted to address, and before we were finished, we had a twelve-page campaign booklet! I should have known then that Ralph liked to do big things. Soon everyone would learn that.

Ralph has led the Borough Council to do so many major projects that it's hard to sort them out, so I won't try. I'll just relate the biggest of the big as they come to mind. We'll start with the Borough Hall, a beautiful building built and donated by Borough industrialist and philanthropist, Joseph R. Grundy. Decades later the building it had fallen into serious disrepair by the time Ralph took office, and he was determined to fix it. The problem was that the Borough had no money for a capital improvement that large. To compound the problem, Ralph didn't just want to do a renovation, he wanted to restore the building to its original integrity following the guidelines of historic preservationists. He also wanted to increase the efficiency of the Borough staff by completely computerizing the building, and to convert the police department into a state of the art law enforcement facility. All of this, of course, would add to the cost. That didn't deter Ralph. He set out to secure grants from a host of sources. He must have been quite persuasive because he assembled sufficient funding to complete the project. Today, the Bristol Borough hall is, without question, the most beautiful municipal building in Bucks County and a model of historic preservation and efficiency.

Turning to another infrastructure/facilities issue, Bristol Borough funded its road repair program the same way Boroughs maintained their roads throughout Pennsylvania, by using annual allocations from the liquid fuels tax assessed on motorists. The allocation was usually enough to do two or three roads per year. The problem was that our roads were in significant disrepair and resurfacing two or three per year would fall woefully short of our town-wide needs. Thinking out of the box, Ralph conceived of the idea to float a bond for the amount necessary **to do all of the roads at once.** The thinking was to use the liquid fuel allocation to make the annual payment on the bonds. By the time the bonds were repaid, the roads would need another resurfacing and the process would be repeated. It was a brilliant idea. The roads were resurfaced, and today, other municipalities are following the lead of Bristol Borough's road program.

During the past eleven years under Ralph's leadership, the Borough has secured almost $13,000,000 in grants to fund major projects like the municipal building mentioned above as well as a comprehensive maintenance facility and related equipment that allows for the efficient provision of services at reduced costs. Bristol also received a $1,3000,000 grant for the installation of ornamental traffic lights synchronized for emergency services.

Time and space does not permit a full recounting of all of the projects undertaken during Ralph's tenure as council president, but what we cannot skip is Ralph's vision, exhaustive work, and perseverance over nine years to put together the $3,000,000 boat dock and pier project on the Borough riverfront. Calling upon the personal relationships and trust he had built with federal, state and county officials like Congressman Mike Fitzpatrick, State Senator Tommy Tomlinson, State Representative John Galloway, County Commissioner Rob Loughery, and Gene Williams of the Grundy Foundation, Ralph was able to secure the needed funding and put together the single most important economic development project in Bristol Borough over the past fifty years. Not only did it maximize the utilization of our greatest natural asset, the river, but it contributed at just the right time following the Small Business Revolution win, to the growing positive buzz about the new, emerging Bristol Borough.

As if all of this weren't enough, Ralph devotes weeks of his summer every year to provide two recreational events that are among the highlights of the season. For twenty-two years he has organized the St. Ann Fair (now called St. Ann-St. Mark Fair) which provides games and rides for children and outstanding food for adults. It is an enormous amount of work and Ralph recruits scores of volunteers to work every night for a week to make it happen. I believe they do it out of respect for Ralph because he leads by example, giving freely of his time. Over the years, the carnival has generated over $1,000,000 for the parish, but I think there is a reward greater than that. Each summer as I watch the smiling, excited kids converge on the event, I can't help but think that, for many of them from lower income families who may not have the resources to take a family vacation, the carnival is the highlight of their summer that will leave fond memories of their childhood in Bristol Borough.

The second event is geared for people at the opposite end of the age spectrum but no less appreciated. Under Ralph's leadership, the Borough Council sponsors an Oldies in the Park/Doo Wop concert that attracts 10,000 people to the Borough Riverfront. Featuring original stars from the past, it is one of the most popular summer events in the county and an excellent marketing tool for the Borough as visitors get to see our beautiful riverfront while enjoying musical memories.

Millions of dollars in grants, far more than any other town in Bucks County, bold, creative problem solving, and an ability to cultivate trust and commitment from major decision makers, these are all part of Ralph's legacy.

Someone once told me that elected officials must have the courage to lead, to follow their convictions, even in the face of severe criticism. No doubt, Ralph faced criticism for every project mentioned and more. The naysayers doubted and preached gloom and doom for the Borough. But each time, the project was completed in exemplary fashion and the bills got paid.

This section of the book deals with those who planted seeds so that later generations may enjoy the shade. We will reap the benefits of the projects that Ralph, his fellow council members, and the Borough's professional staff spearheaded for many years to come. But more than that, his bullishness about Bristol Borough and his bold approach to problem solving makes Ralph DiGuiseppe a true game changer.

Chapter 36- Mycle Gorman

Dale Carnegie once said, "People rarely succeed unless they have fun in what they are doing." (I can't believe I'm quoting Dale Carnegie, but the quote works here). Raising the Bar has had a great deal of success, and I believe it's due in large part because of RTB Board member Mycle Gorman. He is one of the hardest working and remarkable people I've ever met, and he makes things fun. He also makes things happen.

Mycle owns a highly successful design company and works hard at it. But that doesn't stop him from spending countless hours in service to his town. In addition to being the driving force behind Mill Street Crossing and a key player in the design and development of the Bristol Borough Centre for the Arts, Mycle has spearheaded the purchase and acquisition of hanging flower baskets on Mill Street. He's done the same with American flags on the light poles. He supervised the power washing of the sidewalks in a six-block area of the commercial district at no cost to the property owners. He facilitates Raising the Bar's annual Keep Bristol Beautiful flower sale. He decorates the Mill and Radcliffe intersection, wharf and riverfront for the annual Christmas Tree Lighting. He decorates the various facilities we use for our annual Raising the Bar Gala fund raisers, and the transformations of the sites are magical. He serves on the Design Assistance Team to offer advice and supervision to property owners who have qualified for a state commercial façade improvement grant. He donates his services to advise other property owners on the street about their facades. When I say he does these things, he doesn't do them in an administrative sense. I mean he does them in a hands-on, sleeves-rolled-up sense. He leads by example and has earned the respect of the Borough officials whose cooperation and permission he needs for much of this. He's generous. He's donated all of the furniture for Centre for the Arts gallery. He often pays for things RTB is doing when he thinks no one is looking.

Mycle is a people magnet. He makes friends easily and values the people he meets. He's a goodwill ambassador for the Borough. I don't think there is anything he wouldn't do for Bristol. He has sung and danced at a fund raiser. He's cooked hotdogs for little kids at celebrations and for senior citizens at riverfront concerts. As if all of that were not enough, he's the current president of the Bristol Lions Club.

He's quick with a joke or to light up your smoke and there's no place he'd rather be than Historic Bristol Borough. Mycle Gorman has had a profound effect on the appearance of Mill Street and the larger commercial district, and has changed the culture and thinking of the merchants there. Without a doubt, he's a game changer.

Chapter 37- Bernard Mazzocchi

There are some entertainment artists so acclaimed that they are recognized by merely a first name like, Cher, Madonna, Adele, Bono, Elvis, and Pink, just to name in few. In Bristol Borough, say the name Bernard and everyone knows you're talking about Bernard Mazzocchi. Bold, creative, affable, combative, passionate, generous, confrontational, visionary, he is one of the most complicated individuals I've known in public life and one of the most gifted.

In a town where period architecture should be a highly valued asset, Bernard is a poster child for historic preservation. As a developer, he has led by example in demonstrating that one can preserve and restore the architectural integrity of a building while enhancing its economic value. With his many properties, he's been a master in blending style and substance, form and function, art and science.

I'm convinced Bernard is an artist living in a developer's body, and his buildings bear that out. When I was Borough Council President in the 1980s the old fire house across the street from the municipal building was in deplorable condition. In fact, our building inspector at the time indicated that demolition might be our best option. Bernard came forward and offered to buy it and convert it into an office building. Clearly it was going to require a lot to bring the building up to code and retrofit the interior to make it conducive to office space. Bernard went well beyond that. He acid washed the stone, revealing its true character. He installed antique light poles along the sidewalk. He restored the beautiful red firehouse doors, and landscaped the surroundings. Today, the building is an architectural showplace and a valued part of the image of our municipal complex.

Bernard owns numerous properties in Bristol Borough, but his largest and most dramatic work is his restoration of the one-hundred and thirty- year-old Canal Works building. The building was previously used for various industrial purposes. It is several hundred feet long, has three stories and once employed over two-hundred people. Nineteen years in the making, it is a classic illustration of adaptive reuse. Today it houses twenty-five businesses which employ over two-hundred and fifty people.

As his business literature indicates, Bernard specializes in Building the Future Out of the Past. I've seen the wonderful adaption of former industrial buildings in Philadelphia, Camden, Baltimore, and other cities. Thirty years ago, I even flew to Lowell, Massachusetts with a team of Bristol's civic and government leaders to tour the beautiful conversion of former textile mills, and I can say without equivocation, that Canal Works is the most beautiful building in its category that I have ever seen.

For his vision, job creation and on-going commitment to historic preservation, Bernard has earned the title, Game Changer.

Chapter 38- Anna Bono Larrisey

If you want something done, ask Anna Larrisey. Change that. If you want *anything* done, ask Anna Larrsiey. Or, at the risk of hyperbole, if you want *everything done*, ask Anna Larrisey. Those who know Anna are nodding their heads in agreement with that statement. Those who don't will have to trust me because a list of her volunteer activities and longtime contributions to Bristol Borough defy belief.

A champion of Bristol's rich history and ethnic diversity, she is a longtime officer and co-chair of the Celtic Day celebration. She is on the board of directors of the Bristol Cultural & Historical Foundation and a past chairperson of Historic Bristol Day. She is a founding member and past president of the Columbus 500 Foundation. She was also a Founding member of the Bristol Public Schools PTO. In fact, Anna has "found" more things than the guy with the metal detector at the beach I watch all summer, and won more awards than those young, energized Olympic gymnasts we see every four years.

She was recognized by the Bristol Lions as Citizen of the Year in 2000. She was the Leadership Award winner in the 2014 Bristol Fall Classic, and was named Celt of the Year in 2016 by the Celtic Heritage Foundation, an interesting achievement for an Italian.

Anna has made her mark on so many of Bristol's milestone celebrations and events. She was Co-Chair of the St. Mark Church 150th Anniversary Committee, President of the Bristol Borough 325th Anniversary Committee, and Secretary of the Bristol Borough Tricentennial Association. She is the Co-Chair of the Doo-Wop in the Park event that draws nearly 10,000 people to the Borough each year and is the volunteer coordinator of the St. Ann-St. Mark Carnival and Festival.

It must be noted that Anna isn't one of those people who joins things to get her name in a program and then watches from the sidelines. She works! She's like the guy in the circus who sells the tickets, makes the popcorn and then tames the lions. She does it all, and does it well, and gets better with age.

I'd like to share the words of Anna's son, Anthony, taken from his introductory remarks at 2014 Bristol Fall Classic where she was honored.

I see my Mother's volunteerism through the lens of values and vision.

For her values, I believe that it's her caring, generosity and gratitude that are the fiber of service, and something my Mother would say is in all of us.

For her vision, we do it because it's the right thing to do in order to be a leader, in order to provide service to a community, or to preserve the history of a town, or to celebrate heritage.

Hold true to your vision — it's the right thing to do. And then, pass it on.

This, I believe, is the essence of my mother's volunteer spirit.

And that is what makes Anna Larrisey a game changer.

Chapter 39- Donna McCloskey

Back when we were preparing to write our Economic Development Strategic Plan, I knew that tourism would be an important component, and I asked Donna McCloskey to serve on the committee, largely because of her work with the Grundy Museum. In the course of our work, and largely at the suggestion of Donna, we added Greening Projects to our list of action items that should be addressed as quality of life issues that would make Bristol Borough a more attractive place to visit, live or start a business. When we finished our final report, Donna indicated that the greening component was a keen interest of hers and that she'd like to carry the ball on that item. Boy did she ever.

She was instrumental in forming the Garden Club of Bristol Borough. The garden club was formed to educate gardeners and to enhance the public spaces in the borough in coordination and cooperation with the Department of Public Works. The club has planted many trees in the public spaces throughout the borough; the group plants and maintains the entrance ways into town throughout the year, and they have participated in the county's one Million bulb program by facilitating the planting of over 10,000 bulbs in town.

She spearheaded the first organized community garden in Bristol Borough, inspired by her work and background in the Penn State Master Gardener program. The program promotes environmental education as an extension of the university's agricultural curriculum. The community garden was established at the Adam's Hollow Creek on the site of tennis courts constructed by the borough but always underutilized. The first year approximately 25 gardeners joined the garden and by the third year the space available was full with about 150 members each with at least one box.

No project this large is a one-person operation. Paul Stillwagon, who built many of the garden boxes, was a major advocate of the concept from the beginning. Henry Freitag has been a constant presence, advising and encouraging planters, and Shirly Brady, the group's vice president, helps organize and facilitate the socials held at the site.

The community garden has evolved into a peaceful, relaxing spot for gardeners to gather, share gardening tips and build new friendships. Like bicycle paths, dog parks and river access for kayaking, community gardening is the type of Borough amenity that young, first-time homebuyers are attracted to.

When she's not getting her hands dirty, Donna is a highly effective promoter of tourism in the Borough through her work as Executive Director of the Grundy Museum. In her role at the Grundy Foundation, Donna has leveraged the value of the Grundy Museum to attract visitors to the borough by integrating the marketing with other entities in the County that promote tourism. This coordination of resources, other sites, restaurants, etc. has resulted in the creation of a day long itinerary for visitors that would not exist with each site promoting itself as a stand-alone visit.

Wishing to capitalize on one of Bristol's strongest assets, its architecturally significant and well-preserved properties, especially in the Old Town, Historic District, Donna developed the state of the art audio walking tour of Bristol Borough which highlights many of the historic assets and other points of interest. The tour is accessible on most mobile devices.

For her work in promoting tourism and for tirelessly advancing and involving others in the greening component of Bristol Borough's renaissance, Donna McCloskey has been a game changer.

Chapter 40- Ron McGuckin

Pro Bono- denoting work undertaken without charge, especially legal work for a client with a low income.

Pro Bono work is what Raising the Bar is all about-volunteerism. From all of us on the board of directors who give so much of our time, to the volunteers who staff the art gallery, to the people who hang the flower baskets on Mill Street, to the graphic artists who design our images, to the people who decorate for our events, it's all about work undertaken without charge. Of course, that community work extends beyond Raising the Bar, to the Lions and Rotary club members, to the athletic and non-athletic groups that work with kids, to Bristol Cultural and Historical Foundation, to the volunteers at the theater, library and museum, to firemen and first responders, and others.

Having said that, as the definition above indicates, the term pro bono especially applies to legal work for a client with a low income, the kind of skillful, specialized, and otherwise expensive work attorneys do.

Ron McGuckin's Pro Bono work for Raising the Bar takes the concept to an extreme. Simply put, without his generous contribution of time and skills, we would not be able to function. Ron provides the legal counsel for everything we do. It is such a luxury to be able to pick up the phone and get an immediate opinion about an initiative we're about to undertake. That's the easy part. Beyond that, Ron does all of our bookkeeping, which is extensive. He files all legal documents required by the state and federal governments. He deposits revenue from our fund raisers and writes checks to vendors and artists when their work sells. He ensures that we are adequately insured for our buildings, on-going activities and special events. He writes grant applications. He advises artists on legal issues regarding their work. The list goes on.

Ron's importance to the Raising the Bar movement goes well beyond the tasks mentioned above. Ron is a thinker, a visionary, someone who challenges us to reflect upon what can be and then maps out a plan to make it happen. This was true about the Mill Street Crossing project and the Centre for Arts and will manifest itself in other projects still in the conceptual stage. He's knowledgeable about emerging trends and best practices of progressive small towns across America and shares them with our team. He enjoys a wide network of relationships and uses them to advance the Borough. He enjoys the trust and respect of people on all levels of government. Finally, he is an accomplished and engaging speaker and an excellent ambassador for Bristol Borough.

Everyone on our board does exceptional work on special projects as needed. Ron's function is constant. For what he does on a daily basis, for the projects he has brought to completion and for others that are sure to emerge, Ron McGuckin is a game changer.

Chapter 41- Fred Baumgarten

I had never met Fred Baumgarten until 1986 when, as Borough Council President, I was invited to the evening ceremony marking the acceptance of the Grundy Mill Complex and its clock tower into the National Registry of Historic Places. Congressman Peter Kostmayer was the keynote speaker. I spoke as well, as did others from the National Park Service, the United States Department of the Interior and the Grundy Foundation. It was a pretty big deal, and we all sang the praises of Historic preservation

Fred had purchased the building in 1981 and had spent the intervening years restoring the clocktower prior to acceptance to the National Registry. I remember wondering what kind of individual purchases a 335,000-square foot building already over one-hundred years old. It was an enormous and courageous undertaking. I'll admit that I couldn't get my head around the business end of the complex. The maintenance and heating of the building, the number of tenants, the taxes, the logistics of shipping and receiving. It all seemed daunting to me. Maybe that's why my attention was focused upon the more symbolic significance of the clocktower project.

As magnificent as it is from a distance, knowing the specifications of the clock that rises one-hundred and sixty-eight feet above the town make it even more amazing: it four illuminated faces, each fourteen feet in diameter with their massive wrought-iron hands, the intricate internal mechanism, the four iron balconies, the ornate cornice above it, all combine to make it Bristol Borough's most recognizable and treasured landmark. One can only imagine the expense involved in the restoration of the Mill built by William Grundy in 1876.

What has always struck me about the project is that Fred didn't have to do it. The restored clock was not necessary for the successful operation of Fred's business. He did it out of his deep respect for the past, for the Grundy family that built the structure, for the people of

Bristol Borough for whom it was an iconic symbol. He did it for his sense of stewardship, the idea that buildings such as these are not ours only, even when we purchase them. They are a part of history, and we have an obligation to preserve them, to exercise a sense of historic responsibility during the years that they are under our care.

Yes, Fred has created jobs in Bristol Borough, and his building generates taxes in support of our local services, but I prefer to focus upon the symbolic importance his actions hold for the Borough. Imagine if the tower had not been maintained. Imagine it dark and rusting, its glass clock faces broken and unrepaired. Imagine the message it would send if Bristol's tallest and most recognizable structure became a symbol of industrial decay. The stigma it would be for the entire town. Instead, we can be proud that the clocktower is a beacon of light, of vitality, a symbol that the industrial era may be gone, but we're on the cutting edge of adaptive reuse of our historic treasures.

In 1991 Fred added a flagpole and large American flag at the apex of the clocktower, thus enhancing an already marvelous part of our skyline. Today, it remains the most iconic image in town, captured by artists and photographers more than any other. I've written four books, and the clocktower has found its way onto the cover of each, such is my respect for its significance.

For the jobs and commerce he adds to our local economy, for his steadfast commitment to historic preservation, and for his exceptional sense of civic duty, Fred Baumgarten is indeed a game changer.

Chapter 42- The Advisory and Oversight Committee (AOC) "For the Kids"

Raising the Bar wrote an ambitious and multi-faceted economic development plan for the Borough in 2013. In it we addressed nine pillars with almost fifty action plan components that we've pursued and added to since. All were the subject of significant reflection and debate, but nothing generated more passionate discussion than the subject of education. We decided to add a tenth pillar on the subject and this is what we said:

"Nothing impacts the economic viability of a municipality more than the quality and affordability of its school system. A town-wide survey administered by this committee confirmed this assertion."

We went on to add that an effort led by citizen volunteers to support and supplement the efforts of the school district should be launched, much like the effort of Raising the Bar to support and supplement Borough Council efforts. We suggested that a group of citizens should come forward to lead such an effort and added that Bristol Borough's large contingent of retired teachers could form a significant workforce in that regard.

At the time, the Advisory and Oversite Committee for the Bristol Borough Learning Centers was just a year or two old and most of us weren't fully tuned in to what they did. That has changed. The committee has grown in scope and membership and does extensive work to raise finds in support of the Learning Centers at Snyder-Girotti, St. Mark School and Bristol High School. They help fund remedial and enrichment programs like summer camp, family movie nights, field trips, Reading Olympics, the Bristol High School Greenhouse, the Writer's Voice workshop, and more.

Some say Raising the Bar punted when it came to the tenth pillar in its plan, that we ducked the issue. I disagree. We recognized correctly that the educational issue is so large and important that one group couldn't possibly do justice to both. Bristol needs a separate and concerted effort of support for education. Thank goodness for the work done by the AOC. Like any volunteer group, they could use more help, and I still think that more retired teachers could step up. But in the meantime, the AOC is doing an amazing job. Speaking of help, each year the King George Inn, meaning **Robert Strasser, Bruce Lowe and Chef Fabian,** donate ALL of the food, wine and servers for a major AOC fund raiser called *Jazz on the River.* It is well attended and generates somewhere in the neighborhood of $12,000 for the kids. Now THAT'S the kind of help I'm talking about.

The AOC lists twenty members in its program booklet, but I'd like to cast a spotlight on four who have been the public face of the effort and have worked selflessly for its success: **Mary Gesualdi, Amy McIlvaine, Eugene Williams of the Grundy Foundation, and Mayor Joe Saxton.** For their work in providing enrichment and remedial programs for our students, for their fund raising, for shining a light on the need for more citizen involvement in this volunteer effort, and for much, much more, they are true game changers.

Part V

Where do we go from here? My Thirty-Point Call to Action

So how does Bristol Borough fit into the opportunities for small towns mentioned in the introduction? We've had a pretty good ride. The question now is whether we will look back on 2017 as a hallmark year that ushered in a bright new era of accelerated progress or as a flash in the pan whose illumination soon died out. The answer to that question rests squarely with all of us.

The next several months are crucial for Bristol. The victory party is over, and it's time to get back to work. What follows is *a call to action,* a suggested list of projects and initiatives that I think we should pursue. Although many are based on countless brainstorming sessions with our core Raising the Bar team, others come solely from me. All are offered here as a springboard for discussion. You may love some and dislike others. What's important is that we keep talking because our work isn't finished. I believe we're just getting into high gear.

The danger in listing initiatives for consideration is the potential for leaving something out that others may deem important, so let me address that in advance with an analogy. I love James Madison. He was the genius behind the United States Constitution and authored the Bill of Rights, the first ten amendments to that document. But Madison got a little tricky with the Bill of Rights thing. After providing an extensive list of rights in the first eight amendments (more than twenty by my count), he must have gotten tired, because in the Ninth Amendment he simply said there are other rights without ever telling us what they were, in effect leaving it up to us to decide. I'm not kidding, you can check it out. Anyway, that's where I am with this list. There certainly must be other initiatives that Bristol Borough should undertake, but you'll have to decide what they are and articulate them for the rest of us to consider. As for now, I've listed thirty (which is more than Madison offered), so there is plenty here to digest and keep us busy for quite a while.

Before I list them, I'd like to suggest the mindset we employ to address them.

Chapter 43- Patience Ain't no Virtue

Maxima enim, patientia virtus (which is Latin for, patience is the greatest virtue).
I'm not so sure about that.

Whoever said patience is a virtue probably wasn't fully invested in trying to help a struggling town. People tell me I'm impatient, but I'm not. Well, actually, I am. But I'm not impatient for the heck of it. I'm impatient because I sense the tremendous **urgency of now.** We in Bristol Borough fought hard to win the notoriety we received form the Small Business Revolution contest. Now, opportunities are before us in a way that is uncommon in our recent history. We have to seize the moment, live up to our hype, keep the momentum going, recruit more help, implement new ideas and think out of the box, and we need to move **NOW.** And spare me that, "Rome wasn't built in a day" stuff. I don't give a damn about Rome at the moment. I mean, it's my ancestral home and all, and I wish it well, but we've got work to do right here and now.

Don't let the perfect become the enemy of the good.

We all marvel at perfectionists, people who do things meticulously, pay attention to every detail, consider all aspects of a project, and calculate every step along the way to ensure that the end product is PERFECT. The problem with that approach is that it takes too damn long! I've seen projects grind to a halt and good ideas wither and die because of endless planning and calculation. I support the school of thought that says, "Don't let the perfect become the enemy of the good."

I'm not advocating reckless, careless or shoddy planning. I'm simply advising not to stifle yourself in the pursuit of perfection. When you're implementing an idea, plan it, look it over once, maybe even once more, but then **take action.**

Avoid the ABCs of Mission Creep.

This happens a lot. Someone has a good plan to do X and is ready to go. It is a project or activity that can stand well on its own. Then someone suggests there is a **possibility** that related activities Y and Z can be done as well. If you can pull off all three, then by all means go for it. But if adding Y and Z means getting bogged down and putting X on hold for any extended period of time, then experience tells me to go ahead and do X as originally planned and revisit Y and Z later.

Chapter 44- The Call for Action

------So, with that advice in mind, here is my call for action list. ------

Open a Boutique Hotel or Bed and Breakfast- Bristol Borough is in desperate need of a small, seven or eight room lodging facility to host out of town business visitors or tourists in town. We've seen the need for it time after time, especially during the small busies revolution when film crews and Deluxe officials needed to spend time here. But we've also heard it from larger businesses in town who must lodge guests elsewhere. I hope someone from the private sector beats us to it because it will be expensive and a lot of work, but come hell or high water (I'll have to look up the origins of that phrase), Raising the Bar will either facilitate the opening of a hotel facility by attracting an investor or we will do it ourselves as a non-profit similar to our art gallery project. So, whether it is utilizing one of the available buildings on Mill Street or converting a large Radcliffe Street home, this project can and should be done.

Form a Bristol Based Investment Group- Government and non-profits have done a great job for Bristol Borough and will continue their work, but ultimately, our on-going progress will depend upon us attracting private investment. The time has never been better for it than right now. Of course, that has already begun, but we should accelerate the process by leading by example. Bristolians should invest in Bristol. For example, I believe we can find one hundred or so investors in town or nearby, willing to pool their resources, say at $5000 each, to raise a half-million dollars, identify a project and make it happen, for profit! Whether it's opening the bed and breakfast mentioned above or some other project we deem desirable for the Borough, such a group can make a positive impact on our town and receive a modest return on investment. The one-hundred times five thousand formula mentioned here is only one example. It might be ten more affluent investors putting in a larger amount each, or any variation. I'll leave it to others to determine which investment model would work best, but something along this concept should happen.

Partner with Visit Bucks County- We should maintain a strong association with "Visit Bucks," the official tourism promotion agency for Bucks County, Pennsylvania. The staff there has been very good to the Borough. Currently Elissa Baxt and Robin Butrey are Raising the Bar's liaisons to the agency. RTB promotes the restaurant association, the Centre for the Arts and the ethnic festivals for possible inclusion on the Visit Bucks Website or e-mail blasts. Donna McCloskey and Anne Kohn ensure that the Grundy Museum and the Bristol Riverside Theater have a presence as well. Moving forward, it is important to maintain personal relationships with the staff and to know the Visit Bucks submission requirements to ensure Bristol Borough is appropriately represented.

Utilize the Visit Bristol Website- As previously stated, Deluxe has provided us with a beautiful website to encourage people from the region to visit, dine, shop and enjoy the arts, the docks and pier, the waterfront festivals and the canal. RTB has assumed the cost and responsibility for maintaining the site moving forward. It's important to note that the site is intended for visitors and is focused only for the categories mentioned above.

Recruit and Train Tourism and Investment Ambassadors- We're thrilled by the uptick in inquiries we've received from people interested in our town: investors, tourist groups, historic societies, canal advocates, boating enthusiasts, environmentalists, cyclists, kayakers, art groups, and more. They want to explore opportunities in Bristol and make some contacts. The library and museum do a good job with their relevant categories, as does Raising the Bar, but it is difficult to keep up. We need a team of carefully selected and well-trained volunteers to serve as ambassadors for these visitors. People who can provide information over lunch, lead a tour, or direct visitors to the appropriate contact person. Of course, our local realtors field numerous inquiries as well. We should provide them with appropriate literature and brochures that they can distribute, much of which already exists.

Maintain the Leadership Network- Raising the Bar will continue to host bi-annual breakfasts, open to the leaders of every group in town that works toward business promotion, tourism and civic involvement. In addition to providing leaders a chance to interact and share information about upcoming events or activities, we will continue to develop our database of e-mail and Facebook contacts. This can be a vital tool for the rapid spread of information or the mobilization   of   the   town   behind   a   project.

Cultivate a Stronger Relationship with the Lower Bucks Chamber of Commerce. - The Chamber has been a good friend to Bristol Borough, especially during the small business revolution. We should cultivate a partnership with the LBCCC. Justin Saxton of CBM is a member and also doubles as our liaison to the group. We should encourage local businesses to join and invite the Chamber to have a portion of their periodic meetings in Bristol Borough.

Maintain Strong Ties with the Business Department of Bucks County Community College- The College has worked to develop a program for young entrepreneurs and has demonstrated a keen interest in partnering with Raising the Bar to assist aspiring, new or established businesses in the Borough by providing educational seminars and exploring other services. Tracy Timby, Dean of the Business Department; James Sell, Executive Director of the Lower Bucks Campus, and Kelly Sell of the Business Department have worked closely with the Bristol Borough School District as well. All three serve on the Economic Development Sub-Committee of Raising the Bar, co-chaired by Don McCloskey and Joanna Schneyder.

Sharpen the Focus of the Bristol Borough Business Association (BBBA)- Formerly the Mill Street Business Association, the BBBA changed its name a few years back to be more inclusive of businesses town-wide. It has good, progressive leadership under officers like Jimmy Bason, Patty Samules and Cynthia Adams, and can be a very positive and important force in the continued development of the business district. However, it struggles to identify its main functions. At the time of this writing, it has wisely engaged in the development of a strategic plan that will help identify and clarify their role. My bias is toward returning to their previous focus on the downtown business district. The organization should consider the recommendations set forth here regarding expanding store hours, lighting their stores, enhancing their window displays and engaging in sidewalk cleanliness. The association includes a relatively small percentage of businesses. Currently, the BBBA charges dues of $300 per year. They should consider a tiered dues structure to attract and accommodate businesses in their first few years in operation or provide a reduced rate across the board. In either case, they should clearly delineate what services members receive.

Two of their biggest events, the annual car show organized by long time Mill Street activist, Rich Valajeo and the relatively new First Friday festivals organized quite well by BBBA employee, **Shea Cialella**, draw huge crowds to the street. The challenge for shop keepers is to develop strategies to entice those visitors into their establishments.

A word about First Fridays and the team of people, led by Shea Cialella who work so hard to make them a reality. The success of the event measured by the crowds and number of vendors it draws, as well as positive, anecdotal reactions, now make it a seller's market and puts organizers in the position to be more discerning about the quality of vendors admitted to participate.

Expand the Bristol Borough Restaurant Association- The Bristol Borough Restaurant Association was formed at the suggestion of Raising the Bar to promote dining in the Borough, joint advertising, and cooperative projects like restaurant week. It is an informal association with a narrow focus in which members meet to determine their next activity and how much they will allocate for its promotion. Based upon the notion that promoting Historic Bristol Borough as a dining destination ultimately benefits all of our dining establishments, it is open to those facilities that serve dinner, have a seating capacity of at least twenty-five and contribute financially to the joint projects agreed upon. It's current participants, The King George II Inn, Annabella's, itri wood fired, Café Bombay, The Mill Street Cantina, Cesare's Ristorante, the Borough Pub, the Golden Eagle Diner & Restaurant, and The Pines Tavern (we adopted them because of their proximity to the Borough), offer excellent food and an exciting mix of dining experiences. The Association's promotions are aimed at both visitors and Borough residents. As new restaurants emerge that meet the criteria, as they certainly will, they should be welcomed and recruited into the group.

Speaking of new restaurants, it's important to note the level of camaraderie and support Bristol's established eateries showed the owners of itri as they went through the process of opening. Robert Strasser of the King George testified at the Liquor Control Board hearing in support of itri's liquor application. Donnie Petolillo of Cesare's offered frequent valuable advice. Bobby Angelaccio offered to donate kitchen utensils. Tim McGinty of the Mill Street Cantina dined on opening night to show his support. Larry Warren from the Pines Tavern and Brian Erwin from the Borough Pub extended their best wishes. The owners get it. If Bristol Borough becomes a dining destination, it helps ALL restaurants.

Promote Our Smaller Food Establishments- The Borough is blessed with a plethora of smaller food establishments geared toward breakfast, lunch or take out. They could benefit from some form of joint activities or advertising, but the shape and function of such a large group presents an organizational challenge. Raising the Bar should sponsor a kick-off meeting open to all establishments in this category. The purpose of this meeting would be to establish relationships, build a communications network, brainstorm ideas for future joint activities and promotions, and name a leadership team.

Promote Boat Tours of Our Riverfront- Within the parameters of the grant regulations, the Borough should work to solicit proposals from vendors wishing to offer boat rides/riverfront tours from the floating docks. The vendor would pay a licensing fee to the Borough for the right to charge customers, and the fee would be used to offset security costs at the pier.

A Tale of Two Cities- Bristol Borough should resume the previous ties it established with Burlington, New Jersey to engage in joint activities like the popular Taste of Two Cities and joint fireworks. Raising the Bar's Joanna Schneyder enjoys good contacts there, as do Mayor Saxton and CBM's Angelo Quattrocchi. An occasional water taxi between Bristol and Burlington (see above recommendation) might be a worthwhile goal to explore.

Expand the Hours of Our Shops- A widespread concern expressed by residents and visitors is that our stores are not open enough or their hours are inconsistent. Many close just as potential shoppers are returning home from work. Others are closed on Sundays when visitors are more likely to arrive. The dilemma for shop keepers is like the old chicken and egg riddle. Which came first, the chicken or the egg?

A form of this age-old riddle applies to retail merchants on Mill street as well as Main Streets across the country. Do I open my store and pay staff even when there is little foot traffic to generate sales, or do I keep limited hours to reduce costs until things pick up?

This question has never been more important to Bristol merchants than now, when our town is basking in the glow of the widespread positive buzz that accompanied our SBR win and completion of the dock project. We are attracting more visitors, potential business investors and possible home buyers than we have since the boom of the 1950s and 1960s.

The hype presents wonderful opportunities for our town, but those opportunities won't last unless we capitalize on them quickly. There needs to be a sense of urgency among our existing merchants that capitalizes on our recent success. **Store owners need to bite the bullet extend their hours.** Most likely there will be a gap between the extra operating cost associated with extended hours and the increased revenue that will eventually come, but there is no viable alternative. **To make sales, one must obviously be open.**

Improve the cleanliness of Mill Street- The business district needs to improve its curb appeal. We're not hanging the dirty laundry when we state the obvious. Sidewalks get dirty; people litter; cigarette butts get flicked to the ground; weeds grow in summer, especially on a brick sidewalk; it snows in the winter. It's regrettable, but it is the reality of public places. Some proprietors approach these problems as they should, by sweeping, picking up litter, pulling weeds and clearing snow promptly. Others do not, and the appearance of the street suffers from a hit or miss approach. What is needed is a systematic, joint effort to address the problem. So here comes the tough part. **The Bristol Borough Business Association should contract with vendors to provide all of these needed maintenance services to every property on the street regardless of whether or not they are owned by dues paying members.**

At this point BBBA members should take a breath, count to ten, calm down and then continue reading. The objection to this solution is obvious. Why should someone who is responsible pay for those who are dilatory? I've heard this argument for thirty years, and frankly while I clearly understand it, I've lost sympathy for it. So here is why you should.

You should do it because the street, your street, the street where you make your livelihood, looks terrible if you don't. You should do it because you'd be leading by example. You should do it because you want to change the culture of the street. You should do it because you don't want the dilatory to set the standard. You should do it because it is probably more cost effective to do the whole street collectively than what you are currently paying as individuals. Sometimes we just need to be pragmatic in our problem solving. I predict that if the non-members begin to see the services you are providing, they may be more susceptible to friendly persuasion to contribute toward the effort.

Attack the Parking Challenge- Parking has always been a challenge in the Borough. We have 19th century streets with 21st century SUVs and multiple car families. It is a quality of life issue and should be a high priority. Borough Council should appoint a committee to conduct a parking study and make recommendations. I'm not speaking if commissioning an expensive study at taxpayer expense. Unless there is grant money available for such a study, I'd seek the services of the Bucks County Planning Commission to work in conjunction with a committee of appointed borough residents to explore our parking challenges and opportunities. Here are some things we need to take a close look at:

a) Pocket parking- One of my old time civic role models was Vince Profy, Sr. Vince was a Mill Street businessman and a member of the Bristol Borough Planning Commission. He was a long-time advocate of pocket parking, that is, finding or

169

creating spaces in neighborhoods, vacant lots, etc. where the Borough might provide ten or fifteen spaces that are paved, buffered with landscaping and well lit. The Borough did some of that on Pear Street and at the corner of Pond and Lafayette Streets when buildings there were taken down. It did more of it adjacent to the walking path when the rail spur was removed. It should renew this effort ad look for additional opportunities.

b) Parking Authority- At times the creation of new parking spaces will require funding and a system of allocating those spaces. The borough should explore the efficacy of creating a parking authority.

c) Parking at former institutional sites- Bristol was once the home of numerous churches of various denominations. Sadly, in many cases congregations have shrunk to the point where the churches are no longer viable. Some are just barely staying in operation, while others have already closed. For years former Council President Don McCloskey has talked about having a plan in place to deal with zoning issues regarding future uses. While the future use of these buildings may pose a challenge, many present an opportunity right now because they have underutilized parking lots.

d) Shared Use Parking- *This can be defined* as *parking* areas or spaces that are *used* to serve two or more individual land-*uses*. This is when individual land-*uses*, either on the same site or from nearby sites form an agreement to share available *parking* space and/or land developable for *parking* to meet zoning requirements. Currently, this type of parking is prohibited or severely restricted by our zoning ordinance, often with good reason. However, the concept is utilized in many urban areas and should be explored for implementation here. As we grow and attract new investor interest in town, we'll have to think out of the box.

e) Replace commercial district meters with parking kiosks. – A kiosk system is more efficient, more user friendly and easier to provide enforcement. This idea should be explored by the parking committee mentioned above.

f) Mill Street Parking Lot- There are three issues to be addressed here.

    1. The lot is dirty. A process similar to the street sweeper system should be implemented. Once per month vehicles should be required to be moved so that the sweeper can pass. In many cases a visitor's first exposure to the borough is the use of the lot. It should be clean.

    2. There seems to be a growing number of vehicles, trailers, commercial trucks, etc. stored at the lot. This is a parking lot, not a storage facility. This issue should be explored by the parking committee as well.

    3. Parking shuttle use- This idea is explained in more detail under a separate heading.

Give People a Ride- Create a Parking Shuttle System. While the Mill Street parking lot is a valuable asset, in reality much of it is several blocks away from where people wish to go. Our recent successes will only increase the number of visitors to the theater, our downtown restaurants, our riverfront and retail shops. Add to this the current people, often elderly, who visit a doctor's office on the street each day. We need a convenient and efficient system to get people from the parking lot to their commercial district destination.

As a non-profit organization, Raising the Bar, proposes to operate a shuttle system for this purpose. Under the proposal, RTB would purchase, at its expense, a ten or twelve passenger shuttle which would be parked in the municipal garage lot overnight and would follow a tight route that includes most of Mill Street, the commercial parts of Radcliffe and Market and the Mill Street parking lot.

In most cases visitors can be dropped off no more than bock and half from their intended dining establishment, theater or doctor's office. Late night theater goers or diners would have a safe and convenient method of returning to their vehicles. The loop is short enough that the ride should only last a maximum of ten minutes. A fee of $1.00 or $2.00 per trip would be charged to compensate the driver and maintain the vehicle. Restaurants could decide to deduct the cost of the shuttle from a patron's bill upon presentation of a receipt.

This proposal is offered as a point for discussion and is subject to revision.

Sponsor a Volunteer "Speed Dating" Event - Two things became apparent to me while working with service groups and the general public during the SBR contest. Organizations are always looking for new members to join their group but sometimes struggle to find them. At the same time, there are many civic minded individuals who would like to become more involved in town, but don't know where to start. This sounds like a perfect situation for one of those dating match services. We can link these two needs if we make a concerted effort. I suggest that we sponsor a type of speed dating night for potential volunteers looking for a place to hang their hats.

So, picture this scenario. We rent a hall for a wine and cheese reception and invite anyone thinking about getting involved in service to the town. We also invite our relevant organizations to set up information tables and have a representative give a very brief overview of what their group does. Other members might mingle with the crowd, introducing themselves and making a friendly pitch for their organization. As the night goes on individuals may decide to develop a relationship with one of the groups that they find to be a good fit. For those choosing not to make a commitment, we will at

172

least have sent a welcoming and inclusive message to our residents and perhaps sowed the seeds for future involvement. Finally, we will have raised awareness of what our organizations do.

I'm thinking of groups like the Lions, Rotary, Raising the Bar, ethnic societies, the Garden Club, the Teen Foundation, the First Friday Committee, BCHF, the Grundy Library and Museum, the Bristol Riverside Theater, the fire police, the AOC, and others. All welcome new members or volunteers, and all have the ability to empower residents to reach their potential. We can't afford to leave a valuable human resource untapped.

Do NOT Hire a Main Street Manager- This idea surfaces every so often and then fades away, as it should. The concept is great. Put someone on board who is knowledgeable in marketing and grant writing and let him or her work full time for the street. Here are some reasons why it should not happen. First, there simply is no money to pay the salary, and if there was, I'd prefer to spend it on bricks and mortar for specific projects. Second, what Raising the Bar has demonstrated is that we have a wealth of talent in town and people willing to donate their expertise free of charge and our mechanism for recruiting and empowering talent is growing. Third, RTB has had enormous success with grant writing, as have the Borough, library and museum. Finally, the idea smacks of a "let someone else do it," mentality that I think is harmful. We need our own hands-on, skin in the game approach.

Sponsor a "210" Seminar- In 1947, three family owned businesses were established in Bristol Borough and still thrive today. They are Bristol Fuel/CBM, established by the Quattrocchi family; Mignoni Jewelry, established by Carmen and Carolyn Mignoni, and Cesare's Ristorante, Established by John Petolillo, Sr. **Together, they represent 210 years and three generations of highly successful**

business experience. In the case of Bristol Fuel, Angelo Quattrocchi passed on his wisdom to his son Louis who ran the business for years and has since passed it on to sons Angelo and Vincent. John Petolillo passed on is business to son Donnie who now works side by side with his son John, and Carol and Rose Marie Mignoni continue the work started by their parents.

In other sections of this book we've discussed the value of seminars on marketing, utilizing social media, and developing effective websites. But let me throw out this idea. I believe there are valuable lessons to learn from the individuals mentioned above about customer relations, service, hours of operation, hard work and longevity. I'm dead serious when I say that we should sponsor a seminar featuring these individuals for the wisdom that can impart.

Add Another Concert- The Oldies in the Park/Doo Wop concert is one of the highlights of all of the events held at the riverfront, and certainly our biggest draw to town. It is a favorite of mine and many in my age group. It should be continued and a renewed effort should be made to attract attendees to the "New" Mill Street before or after the concert. Showcasing the street in this way can increase the likelihood that the visitors will return to shop or dine at a later date. Distributing promotional cards touting the district to such a large audience presents a good opportunity as well.

What I'm hearing from some of the younger merchants on the street is that we should consider adding a second concert, perhaps in the spring, geared to a somewhat younger audience, part of the demographic we're hoping to attract as regular visitors. My guess is that those who make this suggestion may not fully realize the work and expense involved, and someone would have to step up to carry the ball, but the idea is at least worth of discussion. Let's not underestimate what the advocates might be able to do.

Increase Aid for the Fire or Auxiliary Police- Our special events, concerts and festivals are fun and add to the vitality of the town, but they put a significant strain on those who monitor, supervise or assist with parking. We need to be discerning about how many events we allow and can accommodate, but I'd hate to see us close the door on consideration of any additional events because of the financial and manpower strain. Instead we should make it clear that organizers who propose new events will be expected to cover expenses and contribute to the support of the Fire and Auxiliary organizations.

Say Good-bye to Outside Food Festival Vendors- Almost everyone loves food vendors or food trucks at outside events. I say *almost* everyone because the town's restaurant owners are not big fans, nor should they be. Put yourself in their shoes for a moment. Our merchants provide a service for our town by creating jobs, paying property taxes, donating to local fund raisers, and advertising to promote Bristol. Then when we're going to have a special day that will draw huge crowds to town, we say we're going to buy our food from a visiting vendor. In fact, we often go out of our way to recruit out of town vendors. From an economic development standpoint, it just doesn't make much sense. It certainly runs contrary to our Keep It Local mantra.

Let me be clear; I'm not speaking of our established ethnic festivals on Italian, Celtic, Puerto Rican or African-American days. They are traditions that celebrate our diversity and allow those groups to showcase elements of their culture. The same is true of the annual canal festival, of which food trucks are a significant component. But for all other riverfront festivals, we need a program that gives the people the street festivals they enjoy, while helping rather than hurting our Borough restaurants. I suggest we follow the pattern implemented by the City of Philadelphia for the Penn's Landing riverfront park. They have instituted a system of vendor facilities on the riverfront operated exclusively by Philadelphia eating

175

establishments. The vendors pay a fee for the right to sell and then do what they do best, provide excellent food for people to enjoy. I have no doubt that our restaurants, large and small, and our sandwich and pizza shops can put on quite a food show and keep the business with Bristol Borough vendors. We should give them the chance.

Organize Neighborhoods: For our first Raising the Bar volunteer town-wide cleanup a couple of years ago, our organizational goal was to have people step up to clean a specific area, usually a bock or two in their neighborhood. Our thought was that if we could attract an organizer in every neighborhood, we could do a comprehensive job. We had more participation in some areas than others, but in the end, the day was a huge success.

I remember seeing a photo of Linden Street resident, Robert Harley posted on Facebook later that day. It showed him making preparations for a neighborhood pig roast that was to follow the cleanup. I thought it was a terrific idea. I later got to meet Bob for a beer at the Pines Tavern and asked him about it. He explained that the people on his Linden Street block were a tightly knit group. They partied together, looked out for each other's property, reported suspicious activity, planted flowers, helped each other shovel out from snowstorms, looked after each other's kids, all of the old-time stuff neighborhoods used to enjoy.

It reminded me of a time back in what was probably the late 1970s. One of the blocks on Cedar Street, maybe it was the 300 or 400 block, seemed to enjoy the same camaraderie and neighborhood pride that I was seeing on Linden Street now. The Cedar Street folks even went so far as to enter floats in the annual Christmas parade.

I thought about what a powerful thing it would be if every block or neighborhood followed their lead by getting to know each other better, having neighborhood parties, looking after each other's properties, taking collective pride in where they live, refusing to accept illegal activity on their block, being the eyes and ears of the police, demanding borough actions when a property owner, especially an absentee landlord, does not live up to standards of decency and property maintenance.

I know that much of our RTB attention is focused on the business district, the riverfront and our tourist attractions. We do that because we believe the advancement of those areas will have a ripple effect of economic growth throughout town. We also focus our activities because we can only do so much. But the truth is that we need to work on improving the quality of life for **all** neighborhoods, and that will take the involvement of a great deal of people.

Raising the Bar should sponsor a town wide meeting where neighbors are encouraged to come in groups and attendees can brainstorm about how they might organize their streets. Hopefully someone from each block would sponsor a meeting. I believe people want to do good things. They simply need a vehicle through which to bond.

Streamline the Commercial District Permit Process.

Bristol Borough's Mill Street isn't much different than Main Streets across America. Most are situated in old towns where the idea of regulated density, building use, signage etc. came about AFTER the streets were initially developed. As a result, local government, in this case Bristol Borough Council, with the best of intensions, is faced with the difficult task of writing a "one size fits all" ordinance for a district whose irregular lot lines were drawn almost three hundred years ago, and whose buildings almost always predate original zoning laws.

Zoning ordinances exist to provide for reasonable restrictions on land utilization, building use and signage, with a clear process for application. They are most easily implemented in newer communities where planers can often start with a blank slate and ask developers or property owners to conform to a uniform standard.

177

Here is what currently happens in old towns like Bristol Borough. An applicant applies for permission to utilize some aspect of a property. The zoning officer reviews the request with regard to applicable sections of the ordinance. If it is a use by right, the officer grants it. If it is a use clearly prohibited in the ordinance, the officer denies it and explains that the applicant may apply to the Zoning Hearing Board to seek a variance. Both of these actions are as they should be. But there is a third area that needs a closer look. In many cases an application presents a grey area, a unique situation, often minor, where the application seems harmless enough, but technically may not conform to a provision of the code. In these cases, the zoning officer correctly proceeds on the side of caution, denies the application and again informs the applicant of the zoning appeal process.

Here are the problems with that scenario in a town that is advocating economic development and user- friendly investment options. Zoning Boards meet once a month, and hearings must be advertised in advance. More often than not, an applicant is required to wait for the next hearing which could be three or four weeks away. Once the hearing us held, the Board has a month or so to decide. Then after the board decides, a neighboring property owner has a month or so to contest the ruling in court. Not only that, but an appeal to the Zoning Hearing Board costs $250, an added expense at a time when an aspiring business owner is already most likely strained by other expenses. This fee is understandably applied because the Borough must pay for the advertisement of the hearing as well as the fees for a stenographer and solicitor.

I suggest the Borough needs a quicker, more streamlined and flexible system. I'm not an attorney, and I would leave the details to those who are, but I offer the following general proposal that has been kicked around. The Borough should create a commercial district advisory team that could review an application before it goes to the zoning officer. The team could then determine that the application raises enough significant issues that it does indeed merit closer scrutiny through normal channels. Hence, nothing changes. On the other hand, it could determine that the requested deviation from the requirement is *de minimis* in nature, so minor as to merit disregard because it does not have a negative impact upon adjacent property owners and is consistent with the overall spirt of what the ordinance is attempting to accomplish.

In that case, the team could issue a formal recommendation to the zoning officer that the request be approved. The zoning officer would be empowered to accept the recommendation, issue the permit and thus, expedite the process, or disregard the recommendation, reject the application and follow traditional channels for the appeal process.

Again, I'm not an attorney, but it seems that some form of this concept could streamline and expedite the process, without issuing cart blanc approvals or inflexible denials.

Develop a Plan for Murals and Public Art- There is no doubt that the arts have contributed and will continue to contribute to Bristol Borough's economic revival. As previously stated about the Centre for the Arts, those who predicted that an art gallery couldn't survive in Lower Bucks County, especially in Bristol Borough, were woefully wrong. Not only are we fully subscribed and financially solvent, we've been voted "Best in Bucks" on two occasions and were recently named member of the year by the Arts and Cultural Council of Bucks County. In addition, long before our gallery opened, there was a vibrant group of artists in the Artists of Bristol organization. Put all of that together and it was inevitable that there would be a push for murals or public art in the Borough.

Having worked closely with artists and local government, I know that the concept of murals can be tricky. Of course, art appreciation is very subjective, and murals can be viewed as awful or very well done. Because of the relative permanence of murals, elected officials are understandably skittish about even addressing the topic, thinking it best if the idea just goes away. But I think it would be a mistake to turn away from murals just to be safe. Instead, we should follow the lead of other towns and draft an ordinance that controls them with clear guidelines of size, location, approval process, etc. We should then create a Public Art Review Board (PARB) similar to our existing Historical and Architectural Review Board (HARB), made up of a combination of local artists and residents. Murals would not be permitted without PARB's approval. The use should be granted sparingly.

There are model ordinances out there to review. Philadelphia does a good job, and we have people willing to gather information.

Maximize the Potential of the Canal as a Tourist Attraction and Recreational Asset- Next to the Delaware River, the canal is our greatest natural asset. The lagoon is, in my opinion, the most beautiful section of the entire canal from Bristol to Easton. It's restoration (see Part III) positioned us to utilize it more fully. Fortunately, the well-attended annual Canal Festival at that site demonstrates strong public support for such activities. We should utilize the lagoon and the adjoining Grundy Park more extensively with canoes, kayaks, possibly paddle boats, and informal musical performances.

Bristol Borough is home to the final mile of the Delaware Canal as it once existed. Sadly, most of that final mile is gone, but the site of the southern terminus of the former canal, where it met the river, can and should be an area of high interest to tourists and canal enthusiasts. The circular foundation of the crane that once offloaded cargo from canal boats to larger vessels on the river still remains and is marked by interpretative signage. We should form a partnership with the D & L National Heritage corridor group to seek funding for a more ambitious attraction at the site, perhaps an artistic interpretation or skeletal reproduction of the crane. Finally, we should work closely with the Friends of the Delaware Canal, led by Susan Taylor, to promote the "lower end" portion of the canal.

Support the Mill Street Run as a Vehicle to Attract Business and Tourism- John Mundy has organized this wonderful fall tradition in the Borough for fifty years. Each year it attracts hundreds of participants and spectators. Recently, Don McCloskey joined John to promote the race and expand participation. The race offers a great opportunity to showcase riverfront as well as our commercial and historic districts. Businesses on the street should strategize about how to capitalize on the event.

Get into the Weeds About Expanding the Tax Base & Seeking Grants

"What we have here is a failure to communicate." Paul Neuman, *Cool Hand Luke, 1967*

While there are policy decisions upon which reasonable people can differ, I'm convinced that many disagreements are based upon misunderstandings, misinformation, a basic failure to communicate.

The challenge with economic growth is that it doesn't affect everyone at the same time, and it is difficult to covey the notion that ultimately, we all benefit. It troubles me each time I hear someone say that the economic progress we're experiencing as well as our projected prosperity has no impact on them. They shrug off economic initiatives with the question, "How does any of this help me?" While some may want to dismiss the question because they feel the answer is obvious, we owe it to our neighbors to respond. Besides, the more people we have on board working in harmony, the more likely we'll be successful, so here are some topics I feel need clarification.

Economic development builds the tax base. We all demand services from our local government. We want police protection and emergency services; clean, well-lit streets; efficient trash and snow removal; quality recreation programs, and well-maintained parks and public places. All of this comes at a cost, and those costs aren't coming down. Without economic growth, government has two choices: either cut services or raise taxes. Both options contribute to a downward economic spiral. Reduced services and higher taxes make the town less desirable. Housing values decline and the flight to live elsewhere continues. **The only viable solution for small towns like Bristol Borough is to expand the TAX BASE with new construction or additions to existing construction. The increased revenue from new construction makes government less dependent upon existing tax payers.**

So how do we do that?

While we're pleased with the increased level of investment interest in the Borough, and optimistic that it will continue to grow, we're not yet at a point reminiscent of the Oklahoma Land Rush of 1889, where the area of Oklahoma City went from a resident population of zero on the morning of April 22, to approximately 10,000 by that evening. Really. That's what free lad will do. **Until we reach the point where investors are beating down the door, we need to nurture and encourage investment. We can be flexible and pragmatic without giving the store away or adversely affecting existing nearby property owners in the process. We need to be Bullish on Bristol.**

Sometimes adding to the tax base comes by building one house at a time. As one of the oldest towns in Pennsylvania, our lot sizes are often irregular and a potential builder will require a variance. Now here's the head-scratching part. Sometimes, the very people who complain about higher taxes, complain when someone seeks a modest variance to make a building project viable and thereby generate

182

additional tax revenue. Talk about cutting off your nose to spite your face.

Local Economic Revitalization Tax Assistance (LERTA)

Now that's a mouthful, but it's a pretty big deal. The LERTA program was passed by the Pennsylvania Legislature to empower local governments to do exactly what the name implies, provide a form of tax assistance for commercial developers in an effort to stimulate economic development and long view revenue for the municipalities that implement it. It has been used successfully in Bristol Borough on two occasions, the Lennox renovation project ten plus years ago, and the $14,000,000 Mill Run project now under construction. Here's how it works. Let's say we have a commercial or industrial property that pays $100,000 in taxes per year. The building is underutilized and there isn't much interest in it from investors. Now if a developer came along to expand or renovate the building say to the point where it had doubled its value, it would be reassessed and the owner would then theoretically pay $200,000. That would be great for the town.

The problem arises when there is economic stagnation, when there is little or no interest in a property or where the numbers simply don't work to make a project viable. This is where the Borough, the school board and the county government can grant a ten-year LERTA to make investment more attractive. Here is a simple version of how it works. The investor makes the renovations that increases the assessed value of the property. In year one he pays the original $100,000 tax but pays 0% on the additional $100,000 of the new assessed value. In year two he pays the original $100,000 PLUS 10% of the higher value. In year two $100,000 plus 20%, etc. This continues until year ten when he pays the original $100,000 plus 100% of the additional $100,000 to equal $200,000. In addition, over the ten years, each time taxes are raised by any of the taxing bodies, the property owner receiving the LERTA plays the increase on the original $100,000 just as anyone else would. The temporary break is only on the new assessed value.

The tax break over those years is what theoretically makes the original project viable. In my view, it's a great program and a no brainer for taxing bodies to grant. The problem is that each time it comes up it is faced with opposition from individuals who operate under a misconception. They think the Borough is losing tax dollars or that their taxes will rise because the commercial property is getting a break. Neither point is correct.

The granting of a LERTA assumes that a project will not take place without it. Therefore, the taxes waived would never be collected anyway because the project wouldn't happen. You can't lose tax revenue that you don't have, and without the incentive you wouldn't have it. It makes pretty good sense, which is why the legislature created this incentive tool.

By the way, there is another very significant benefit to granting a LERTA. By making an economic project viable we are paving the way for more jobs which otherwise wouldn't exist.

LERTA's are granted in0frequently because of the scale of the project involved. But I hope we'll have a better understanding the next time an opportunity comes along.

More on how economic develop helps all of us.

The day we stop moving forward is the day we start moving backward. Economic growth stems the tide toward economic decline. **It maintains or increases all of our property values. It raises investor confidence and increases the likelihood that our young people about to start out on their own will make their home here. It heightens the interest of those outside the Borough to consider buying here as well. Our population has decreased over the past** twenty years, and that's not a healthy sign. We need to reverse that trend.

Economic development **creates jobs**. In the short term, it puts local contractors to work. In the longer term, it creates the jobs necessary to maintain the business being developed or expanded. Some of those jobs, like many found in the businesses at Canal Works, Grundy Commons or the Lenox Building, are good paying positions, the type that can support a family. Others are more modest paying part time positions like retail clerks, waiters, waitresses and receptionists. When we talk about job creation, critics often scoff at the latter category and apply little importance them, and that's foolish. They should talk with people looking for a few extra hours of work in a second job to supplement their income, or senior citizens looking to supplement their pensions. And they should talk to high school kids looking for their first jobs.

I don't think we focus enough on the long- term value those jobs provide young people beyond the income they earn. They learn the importance of responsibility. They gain a sense of how business works. They build their resume for college acceptance or future employment by documenting their dependability. When one reads about the inner cities where unemployment among young people is more than twenty-five percent and idle teen-agers see little opportunity, it's easier to gain a deeper appreciation for the creation of any type of employment. And for older people, part time employment helps contribute to their sense of worth and belonging. It keeps them moving, and most likely improves their health.

Drive Home How Grants Help Us All.

Here's another source of misunderstanding. The federal, state and county levels of government offer specific grants for projects on a host of categories: environmental, recreational, economic development and more. They are usually competitive and have

185

specific requirements. The money must be used for the very narrow purpose intended. Over the years, Bristol Borough has been very successful in securing grants and the current council, under the leadership of Council President Ralph DiGuiseppe, Borough Manager Jim Dillon, Solicitor Bill Salerno and Kurt Schroeder of Gilmore Associates, has literally done an astonishing job in securing millions of dollars of grants for open space, the boat docks, environmental remediation, traffic signalization, road improvements and more. All of this contributes to the quality of life and infrastructure of our town.

Nevertheless, there are complaints. One common complaint based on a misconception is, "Why are they using the money for X? They should be using it for Y?" The answer, of course, is that there were no grants available for Y. They are using the money for the required purpose of the grant. They have no choice.

Another complaint is based not on a misconception, but on a difference in philosophy. Some say that federal and state government spends too much and many grants should be eliminated. And until they are, we shouldn't apply for them. Let me say that I disagree with that position 100%. I'd say 1000%, but there is no such thing. Each year our tax dollars flow to the federal, state and county coffers which are then allocated in their budgets. Part of that allocation is for the grants we are discussing. In other words, the money we apply for is in part, our money. I want every possible dollar flowing back to Bristol Borough. We have one of the lowest per capita income levels in the county. I'll be damn if we will turn down available grants that can help our town advance in order to make a philosophical point. In my view, not applying for grants available to us would be governmental malpractice.

Make This a Time for Healing- Bristol is a tough town, with tenacious, scrappy fighters who get up when they are knocked down. It's one of our strongest assets and part of what helped us scratch and claw our way to winning the Small Business Revolution. Unfortunately, some of these traits often carry over to our local politics. We can go at each other pretty hard, and the wounds that are opened during political campaigns often don't heal. Instead, they become the source of a recurring cycle of bitterness and infighting moving forward. Of course, all of this is disruptive to our rate of progress.

This may be a time when the cycle can and should end. We had a strongly contested local election virtually right in the middle of the final days of the Small Business Revolution experience. Three out of four borough council seats and the mayor's office were contested by two opposing slates, all good people on both sides, seeking a voice for our future direction. In the end, all of the incumbents won by comfortable margins, thus reaffirming the town's endorsements of where we are going and how we're trying to get there. However, an important development to emerge from this election is that the winners managed to win without mounting a single personal attack against their opponents. I think the message the voters sent was that they not only endorsed the programs being implemented, they also endorsed the positive aspect of the campaign.

I believe this can be a time for healing, a time when we put personal animosities and past rivalries aside and truly work together to do the business of Bristol. This is especially important now when we have an opportunity to capitalize upon our recent SBR success to make significant strides forward. To be sure, there will always be differences on policy, and they should be the subject of spirited, civil debate. But the time is right for civility and reconciliation. I hope we achieve it.

Part VI

Glory Days

Most people are familiar with Bruce Springsteen's song, *Glory Days*. It a great sound, performed as only The Boss can deliver, but the lyrics tell a sad story of people whose best days are behind them. They live in the past, holding on to their memories.

Springsteen reminds us:

Glory days, well, they'll pass you by

Glory days, in the wink of a young girl's eye

Glory days, glory days...

We **can't** let that be us, and if I know the people of Bristol Borough, it **won't**. We won't look back at 2017 as the year we hit our zenith. We'll view it as the year we went from high gear to overdrive and kept reaching for more.

Raising the Bar is always looking for people to donate their time, talent or treasure to town projects. I hope each of you who read the ideas in the **call to action** find one you'd like to get behind and contact a Raising the Bar board member listed in the front of this book to tell us you'd like to get involved. We'll do our best to put you to work.

We realize life's circumstances or demands on one's time sometimes prevent people from becoming as involved as they'd like to be. In those cases, we hope you'll consider supporting our projects by purchasing a ticket to one of our events or by sending a modest donation to our non-profit organization, Raising the Bar, PO Box 2126, Bristol, Pa. 19007.

At the very least, I hope you'll spread the word and cheer us on because we're all in this together and we need all the help we can get.

The End.

Which is really the beginning.

Appendix I

Not by Faith Alone

Religious Organizations as Community Leaders

Thirty-five or forty years ago, the pastors of the various churches in town met periodically to discuss issues of common interest, one of which was involvement in community projects. I remember one year in particular when they fully embraced the Borough's spring, "Clean-up, Paint-up, Fix-up" campaign. As a member of St. Mark Parish, I went to a meeting sponsored by Father Moore and Father Evans, two young and enthusiastic priests at the parish who were planning the role of St. Mark's in the program. At the time, the Bristol train station platform was an old wooden structure with unsightly, peeling paint, and SEPTA had little interest or funding to do anything about it. So, Moore and Evans had adopted the dilapidated train station platform as their project, and were recruiting people to help scrape and paint it. I remember Father Moore coining the slogan, "If it's apeeling, it's appalling." It was corny, but effective. A score of people converged on the platforms that day and painted.

The experience was fun and gratifying, and left a lasting impression on me about the role church organizations could play or are playing in Bristol's revival. Over time, the joint meetings of pastors went by the wayside as some of our more established churches experienced a decline in membership and are just barely hanging on, but others are thriving and they constitute a valuable asset in our collective efforts to improve our community. While developing the Raising the Bar concept, we never lost sight of the importance of reaching out to them to solicit their support for special projects as they arise.

To accentuate their importance, I've invited a sampling of pastors to share reflections about the valuable role they play in community service.

Dr. Matt and Michele McAlack
Pastor of Youth and Family Ministry
Calvary Baptist Church

Reaching and empowering families to create a dynamic and sharing community is one key to raising the bar in Bristol Borough. During the past several years, Calvary Baptist Church has enjoyed being an active member of the Bristol Borough community and has been instrumental in sparking progress toward this goal. The church's involvement in several pivotal events have helped emphasize the importance of family time together. Annual events in Bristol Borough include the Martin Luther King Day of Service, Bristol Family Movie Night, "Trunk or Treat", Turkey Dinner Giveaway, and the Bristol Christmas Parade. The church also helps raise the bar in Bristol by helping those who are under-resourced. We host Code Blue to house the homeless on cold nights, aid families with low income through an active community food pantry service, and also provide a monthly community hot meal for the homeless and those in need.

The annual Martin Luther King Day of Service gives families the opportunity to serve together to honor the legacy of Dr. Martin Luther King. On this special day of service, families gather at Calvary Baptist Church for a short program and then they get busy as they take part in distributing invitations for the community to take part in a food collection to benefit several local food banks in the borough.

Bristol Family Movie Night at the newly renovated Bristol Wharf offers free popcorn, free drinks, and a popular movie under the stars. It's the perfect place for the family to spend time together building memories as they bring their beach chairs and blankets and enjoy time with neighbors and friends.

"Trunk or Treat" in the church parking lot is a highlight of the year! Hundreds of children and their families come in costume to witness the spectacle of dozens of cars, each decorated to the hilt and each one offering candy treats to the kids. A hook and ladder fire engine, music, photo booth, and free hot dogs are all also part of this special Halloween event. It has already become a Bristol tradition for many families to experience a fun, creative, and safe atmosphere on Halloween.

The Turkey Dinner Giveaway is made possible by generous donors in Bucks County. Families who are in need receive a full turkey dinner including a frozen turkey, all the fixings, and even a tasty dessert. Families from Bristol Borough are invited to come and help distribute the dinners and to enjoy a community lunch in the Calvary Baptist Youth Center. About 250 meals are donated and hundreds come to enjoy the community lunch.

Calvary Baptist Church has enjoyed showing its support and love for the community by preparing a float for the parade. The Bristol Borough Christmas Parade is held each year on the Saturday after Thanksgiving. The parade is a beautiful representation of the diversity and creativity that raises the bar in Bristol Borough.

It is delightful to see the positive changes that are happening in Bristol as we partner together to "raise the bar" for families and friends of Bristol Borough. It is because of the concerted effort of so many that the spirit of this blue collar, hard-working town is now showing off its pride to the world. Calvary Baptist has been part of this community for nearly 80 years and is proud to see that Bristol's best days are still ahead.

Gary Alloway

Pastor, Redemption Church of Bristol

When I first stumbled into Bristol Borough in 2008, two things struck me. First, the town was beautiful. It had a classic main street filled with historic storefronts opening up to the Delaware River. And second, the town was empty. Half the storefronts were vacant, the businesses were struggling, and on this particular day, not another soul was out on the street. Into this silence something stirred in me, an inner voice saying, "You need to do something here." That next year, we started Redemption Church of Bristol with the explicit mission of helping to breathe new life into Bristol Borough.

As we went out in Bristol, we realized that the biggest obstacle the town faced was not money or jobs or lack of events. It was despair. People had given up. "This town used to be great." "We've tried that before and it didn't work." I was specifically told, "This town eats pastors alive, so watch out." We soon came to see that the biggest thing Bristol needed was hope. Without hope, nothing would change.

Churches and other faith-based organizations are in a great place to bring hope because we believe in stories of hope. We believe that even if all the data says otherwise, even if every trend line is pointing in the wrong direction, a place and a people can be made new.

But spreading hope doesn't just involve going around and telling people to be hopeful. It involves doing a lot of stuff. Only when people see new things happening will they begin to believe that change is possible. The challenge, though, is that when a town has been beaten down for too long, most new ideas will fail. Most new endeavors will be under-supported and underfunded with a hundred naysayers telling you, "That will never work here." But if you persevere in hope through the inevitable failures, you will begin to change people's minds. Eventually, the right people will see what is happening, get on board, and things will begin to move.

About this time, you will also find that you are not so alone, but there are others who have been working tirelessly in hope, often in parallel to you. And if you can stay committed to the vision rather than the enlargement of your organization, you will get the opportunity to form partnerships, which will take you much farther than you could ever get on your own. One of these key partnerships for us was Raising the Bar, who would work with and promote anyone who wanted to help Bristol grow. Because they were centered on a vision, rather than organizational goals, it allowed everyone to join in. What a joy to work side-by-side with businesses, nonprofits, and committed citizens on cleanup days, service projects, and of course, the Small Business Revolution. The whole town was able to gather in community around a vision of hope. As the old saying goes, "It's amazing what you can accomplish when you don't care who gets the credit."

All of these principles came together for us in the creation of First Fridays in Bristol. When Redemption got started here, no one hung out on the main street at night. As a result, none of the businesses stayed open in the evening. As a result, no one hung out on our main street at night. It was a vicious cycle. Our vision was to create a monthly arts and music night on the street where for at least one night a month, we could turn the cycle the other way.

In the summer of 2011, we tried it and failed. In 2013, we tried it again and fell short. In 2014, we tried one more time. I will never forget being out in the middle of town with less than 20 people trying to drum up energy on an empty street. It was a stupid hope to keep going. But in 2015, a few people from the business association got a hold of the idea and put way more time, energy, and passion into the project than I ever could. Now two years later, First Fridays in Bristol are one of our town's biggest draws, gathering thousands of people to our main street during the summer months.

Sometimes hope means looking like a fool. It means being the only person out on an empty main street believing that what is dead can be made alive again. But if you are stupidly hopeful, eventually despair can be broken and new life comes. Churches and faith-based organizations can do many things to lift up a town. But we are always called to be people of hope.

In 8 years in Bristol, we have planted a church, helped start businesses and community events, and gotten a few dozen young people to move into Bristol, buy homes, raise kids, and invest in this town. Every one of our successes has come after repeated failures with an army of skeptics whispering in our ears. But we do not give in to despair. We live in hope. We live into hope. And we give it away to all who want to be part of the party.

Rev. Dennis M. Mooney
Pastor, St. Mark Parish

The year of 2017 is going to be remembered as a banner year for Bristol Borough. The year was (and continues to be) great in so many ways. Yes, we had the celebrations and the hoopla and the glitz and the glitter. But what matters most is the magical sense of pride that our people feel. The pride that says that this town in which we live is something special. Our people make this town what it is and what is shall continue to be.

I have had a slogan for a couple of years about St. Mark Parish and St. Mark School . . . ***St. Mark's is the Best in Bucks.*** Let me now bequeath that slogan to Bristol Borough . . . ***Bristol Borough is the Best in Bucks*** and in keeping with what Deluxe Corporation has done . . . ***Bristol Borough is the Best in the Whole Country***.

Let me share with you a letter that I wrote to Amanda Brinkman at Deluxe Corporation . . .

November 30, 2016

Ms. Amanda Brinkman
Deluxe Corporation

Dear Ms. Brinkman:

We have learned of the good news of the Small Business Revolution and of Deluxe Corporation. I understand that

---

there is a significant grant being considered. This would certainly be a wonderful asset for Bristol Borough.

Since our founding in 1845, St. Mark Parish has always been an integral part of Bristol Borough. We continue today as a vibrant Parish and we are especially proud of our two hundred and thirty student elementary school.

I am confident that our parishioners, including our school students, would want to become heavily involved in whatever programs the Small Business Revolution would institute.

Sincerely,

Rev. Dennis M. Mooney

The point here is that almost a year ago, I and many others felt and somehow knew that something special was in the works. We didn't know for sure what it was or when it would happen but we knew that good news was around the corner.

Now, about the involvement of St. Mark Parish in the Small Business Revolution. Just a couple of years ago, our Parish decided to completely upgrade and modernize our school computer program. Through the efforts of our staff people and of our very generous donors, we became absolutely hi-tech.

This turned out to be fortuitous when the Small Business Revolution came along. You will recall that voting in the SBR had to be done on computers, tablets or smart phones. Not everyone had access to those devices so we decided to open our school at night to ensure that a vote would be cast each day from every device we had. We also sent literature home with our students urging their parents to vote on every device every day. Finally, we included a message in our announcements after Sunday Mass, asking parishioners to vote. St. Mark Parish was fully invested in the contest.

There have been a host of other positive events - all that Raising the Bar has done, the visit from the Clydesdales, the rebirth of Mill Street, the new dock facility. All of these things make Bristol Borough a great place in which to live and a great place in which to work. And not to mention, a great place to visit.

As mentioned earlier, St. Mark Parish has been a part of Bristol Borough since 1845. Aside from our obvious pastoral responsibilities, we have always had a keen sense of community involvement. That involvement, that commitment will continue be a core part of our existence going forward. It's great to be a part of Bristol Borough.

Appendix II

Our Small Business Revolution Friends from Around the Country

One of the most gratifying things about the Small Business Revolution experience was getting to interact with other competing towns across the country. We saw their promotional videos produced by Deluxe for the contest, spoke to their representatives during contest conference calls, and read the posts of their citizens on the SBR Facebook page.

The Deluxe team had traveled 10,000 miles to conduct interviews and do the film shoots for the various towns. What the videos revealed is that although we were thousands of miles apart, we were remarkably similar in our challenges, aspirations, and the spirit of our citizens.

Just as Deluxe believes that small businesses can benefit from the experiences of the businesses featured in their video production, I believe small towns can benefit by sharing their successes and best practices. I'm hopeful we can build upon that concept moving forward.

To get the dialogue started, I've invited representatives from some of the towns we competed against to submit a note here. I hope it is the beginning of things to come. Small town leaders everywhere will see in their messages a commonality of hopes, dreams and challenges.

The first note is from **Patty Brown from the Red Wing, Minnesota** Chamber of Commerce. It is followed by notes from **Dave Perkins from Woodland Park, Colorado** and **Alexander Henderson from Kingsburg, California, and Jessica Palumbo from Frostburg, MD.**

You'll remember that Bristol Borough was neck and neck with Red Wing in the final hours of voting. A few days after we learned we had won, someone posted on Facebook a video of the Red Wing gathering when the SBR Season 2 winner was announced. There they were in their theater, dressed in red, anxious and excited, with balloons everywhere. Then, there was a collective gasp when they learned they hadn't won. Their level of disappointment was obvious. But within seconds, I witnessed one of the most gracious displays of class and sportsmanship I've ever seen, as the entire audience broke into applause. They were applauding us. They had worked every bit as hard as we had and utilized every resource at their disposal, but despite their disappointment, they had the grace and style to applaud our success.

I will never forget that scene. It solidified my belief that whether we're from Red Wing or Woodland Park, or Kingsburg, or Georgetown, South Carolina, or Marietta, Ohio, or Frostburg, Maryland, or North Adams, Massachusetts, we're all in this together.

The final message is from Christine Flohr, from Wabash, Indiana, the Season 1 Winner of the Small Business Revolution-Main Street contest. Christine asked to share a letter she wrote to Lee Schram, the CEO of Deluxe one year after their win.

Red Wing Minnesota
Patty Brown, Executive Director/President
Red Wing Area Chamber of Commerce

Red Wing, Minnesota is a year-round destination for outdoor adventure, romantic getaways, history buffs, art lovers, business and meetings & conventions. It's a pretty drive, just 55 miles from downtown Minneapolis and 50 miles from Rochester. Red Wing is nestled along the banks of the mighty Mississippi River beneath towering limestone bluffs. Our beautiful historic downtown buildings and homes have been well preserved to make Red Wing the most picturesque quaint river town. Red Wing provides a playground for all ages to live, shop, work, hike, walk, bike, ski, fish, boat and more!

However, Red Wing's downtown is made up of several small businesses that are finding it hard to compete in today's global marketplace. Being involved in the Small Business Revolution has made a lasting impression upon the community of Red Wing and every business here. The Small Business Revolution impacted Red Wing in many positive and unexpected ways. It ignited a spirit of community involvement and in our businesses, both large and small that has not been experienced in Red Wing's recent history. It was so exciting to see the community embrace our businesses and rally to the very end of the competition to demonstrate the importance of small businesses as the lifeblood of our community.

In the days and weeks leading up to the final announcement, Red Wing, the state of Minnesota with support from national and international friends and organizations, helped propel us into the spotlight. The Small Business Revolution highlighted several small businesses, which resulted in many local people discovering them as well. We know that retail traffic increased and that our small businesses learned the power of social media as a part of their marketing mix. Retailers gained hands on experience of promoting their business via social media and were able to connect it to their bottom line. They supported each other in new and creative ways along with their followers. Many retailers became more aware of their storefronts and the role that they played in inviting shoppers into their business and how their marketing materials and packaging impacted their brand. These marketing efforts enabled the businesses to take previous training and information that has been presented in seminars by the Red Wing Area Chamber of Commerce and Downtown Main Street and apply it during the Small Business Revolution in ways they have not done in the past.

Red Wing gained more than $1 million in media and press coverage and thousands of posts and views on social media platforms. Now the world has had a more in-depth introduction to Red Wing and we have enjoyed increased visitors to the area as a result. More people are staying in hotels, eating in restaurants and shopping in our unique stores. They are personally experiencing what the Small Business Revolution highlighted during the contest.

In the months following the contest, the ripple effect continues to touch our businesses and community and shape the community in new and different ways. It is rare that a day goes by without someone mentioning they voted for Red Wing during the contest. People have embraced and continue to support our small businesses. The Small Business Revolution is now a part of the fabric of the Red Wing community conversation on multiple levels; with the City of Red Wing, local businesses and organizations and those that live in and love Red Wing. The contest experience has helped shape discussions on how to build on the momentum of attracting more successful small businesses and how to create efficient systems to assist them and also retain our existing businesses and provide them help in the future. Even though Red Wing didn't win the actual contest, our community had so many "wins" in other ways, we know we will continue to see the positive effects for years to come.

Woodland Park Main Street / Small Business Revolution 2017
Dave Perkins

Woodland Park, Colorado, sits at the foot of Pikes Peak, a 14,000-foot mountain, famously known as *"America's Mountain"*, and the literal birthplace of *"America, The Beautiful"*, the beloved song. The surrounding views are breathtaking and the weather spectacular (i.e. Richard Harris singing "Camelot"). Our 8,500' elevation is ideal for people wishing to beat the heat, desiring to indulge in year-round color, and wanting peace and tranquility.

The rich and diverse history of Woodland Park is as broad as most towns, filled with larger than life characters, who called it home over the past 125+ years. Our version of the "Wild West" recently died in the early 1950's, but the spirit of those early pilgrim's, adventurers, and risk-takers, exists today and is as strong now as the mid 1800's.

Although the 1950's are nearly 70 years behind us, one only has to wander outside to time travel to a not so distance time, to revisit our frontier birth. Cowboys and Indians, brothels and trains, silver and gold miners, pioneers and presidents, each riveted deeply in our history. A ten-minute drive outside of town alone, presents a wilderness full of elk, bears and mountain lions, and the imagery of Indians, ranchers, pioneers, cattle rustlers and scoundrels.

The largest obstacle facing our business community is equally the greatest opportunity for growth. As a bedroom community to Colorado Springs, 12 miles away, a high percentage of commuting residents shop Colorado Springs, shunning local businesses. Woodland Park is not an inclusive one-stop shopping town wherein residents fulfill all needs. This is a loss of sales tax revenue and employment potential.

Woodland Park is not a destination city, where tourists spend a long weekend or week, but is rather a drive-through nuisance for the 28,000 cars daily traveling through the heart of the downtown, to points 60 to 75 miles away. The close proximity to home, does not justify the "pit stop" and lost time.

People love to shop but they must have a compelling reason to explore the possibilities. Many people living in the area, do not know the gems we possess. Our business owners must understand the need to tirelessly promote their business through social media as well.

We desperately need help getting to the next level.

Woodland Park growth is hindered, in part, by an "identity" crisis regarding the on-going debate whether to be a sleepy mountain town, bedroom community or self-employment hub. Woodland Park has dreamt of being a ski town and tourist town, although some vehemently object to anything other than a lazy 70's mountain town. That era is long gone.

This younger generation demands a different set of amenities, even from previous younger generations, creating a natural chasm between old and new, young and old. Meanwhile older generations dislike traffic and waiting in line, each of which, most would view as a sign of progress.

A highway by-pass was fought years ago by downtown business owners fearing decreased store-front traffic would result in a loss of sales and cause business closures. Forty years later the City is inundated with traffic, yet downtown business struggles to get traffic to stop and shop. A downtown dissected by a U.S. highway is a paradox - a plethora of travelers, with no time to stop.

Woodland Park has seven acres of undeveloped vacant land in the middle of town and no unbelievable ideas on how to use it. There is only one chance to get this development "right", and raises the question "What is the highest and best use?" We need dreamers and visionaries to maximize the socio-economic potential of this land.

If asked the question and upon careful thought, townspeople want the same thing – a better quality of life, but as with every town opinions differ defining "quality". Quality can range from better parking to less traffic, to more parks, free wi-fi and teen employment, to arts festivals and philharmonic concerts.

The Small Business Revolution experience brought the needed attention to both the beauty of and plight of our small business. Throughout the process, the town was abuzz about the opportunities, questions raised, ideas formulated, and *"If only this could happen"* dreams unleashed. But how do we maintain that focus and energy?

The many volunteer groups and civic groups tirelessly promote and improve the town, through social, cultural, and economic events, and developing points of interest. Our business owners strive to increase curb appeal and service. And these efforts do, and are slowly effectuating change in Woodland Park. Our town is even more attractive to outsiders, evidenced by the recent surge in new home construction and an expanding main employer.

America is at a crossroads, wherein technology clearly rules the future, intersecting with the demographic shift from baby boomer to millennial. Town leaders and business leaders alike, must anticipate this inevitable change with the future in mind, or be lost to using the same tired age-old solutions that consistently failed the past 50 years.

The era of hiring outside consultants to "solve problems" should be dead and gone, since they perpetuated the same failed solutions. Today is the era of reinvigoration, where three to five people at a time, determine to take ownership of their streets, downtown and community and rely upon themselves vs. outsiders. **And for this new attitude, we have the Small Business Revolution to thank.**

Our Main Street organization is working with CDOT (Colorado Department of Transportation) to both increase pedestrian safety on U.S. Highway 24, while simultaneously increasing beauty. Pedestrian safety is the number one reason given why people dislike our downtown.

2020 Vision is a newly-formed group of special individuals, undertaking the task to initiate change by inspiring and encouraging entrepreneurs, creating educational seminars to incorporate social media marketing, and provide support need by business owners.

Another group recently formed the Teller County Film Commission to attract filmmakers to our area, and possibly create a nationally recognized film festival. The concept is so new, the economic impact cannot be measured at this time. However, a producer has already committed to three films. This in just the first three weeks in the life of the film commission!

Nonprofit organizations and civic groups are stepping up their game, and garnering more energy, and refocusing their mission and vision statements. Individuals are thinking "outside-the-box" and testing age-old axioms. Both individuals and groups are putting aside differences and collaborating, to "make things happen."

An unfortunate attitude of *"I'm OK why should I care"* can prevail, but neither prepares one for the future nor encourages the requisite risk-taking attitude to profit from the future. Further, a "head in the sand" attitude spells near certain doom for the owner/entrepreneur unable or unwilling to plan for future risk, even as untold business opportunities, have yet to surface. City leaders must also prepare utilizing this same risk attitude.

While Woodland Park's awakening will never equate to the "awakening of a sleeping giant" (i.e. America after Pearl Harbor), we may yet be that hibernating bear, finally realizing its time to get out and eat, after deciding the future begins today.

Woodland Park has a solid business community foundation upon which to continue building. The great challenges set before us present great opportunities. We are eager to embrace these challenges with a renewed vigor and a keener vision, and to elevate Woodland Park.

Kingsburg, California
Alexander J. Henderson, City Manager

Many of the finalist towns talk about how being a part of Small Business Revolution (SBR) brought them closer together. It was different for Kingsburg. We have been a tight knit community since our inception in the 1800's. What SBR did do was create excitement. We are overshadowed by bigger, more aggressive cities. This sort of notoriety never happens for us, not in California and certainly not in the United States.

One might think that being in a state which houses over 12% of the U.S. population would have given us an advantage in voting. I think it actually worked against us. Kingsburg is an agricultural town of 12,000 residents nestled in the San Joaquin Valley of California. With Los Angeles south of us and San Francisco north of us we don't get a lot of attention. The 'state pride' angle doesn't really work here.

During the voting process, we did, however, leave it all on the proverbial field. Our strategy was intricately varied with multiple levels of resources. We opened up voting suggestions to the public, received a bunch, and implemented every single idea we could get our hands on. While disappointed, we don't think we could have done anything differently. It just wasn't meant to be. Frankly, making it to the finals felt like winning in and of itself.

Just weeks after learning we weren't the winner, the California Chapter of the American Planning Association (APA) announced that Kingsburg had been selected for pro-bono planning assistance. We were the first community in California selected to receive this assistance. Six seasoned City Planners immersed themselves here for four days. As a result, we received a detailed, step-by-step report on how to revitalize our downtown. We immediately went to work implementing their recommendations.

Our Roots

In 1921, ninety-four percent of the population within a three-mile radius of Kingsburg was Swedish-American, giving the community the nickname of "Little Sweden." Most of the Swedes were directly or indirectly involved with agricultural.

We've held onto that heritage by keeping the Swedish motif throughout the entire city. When Amanda Brinkman and her Deluxe team arrived, we explained that we are a California city with midwestern values. They wanted to know what that meant. We explained that we're an agriculturally driven community, where people help each other, take care of each other and are supportive. In agriculture it takes many, many hands to go from planting to harvesting. We all work closely together and the children learn this early on. Our schools are not divided by location or socio-economics. Instead, schools are divided by grade levels. All of the kindergarteners attend one school. All of the first graders attend another school and so forth. You graduate from high school with the same kids you have known nearly your entire life.

Our Future

With retail shifting to online purchases, we knew we would have to pivot in order to maintain our downtown. The first time a bus-load of tourists pulled to the side of the road so that the passengers could get out and touch the blossoms in an orchard, it became obvious that agree-tourism would be a viable way to help support the local merchants.

With the observations from Small Business Revolution coupled with the suggestions from our guest planners, Kingsburg will be able to once again transform our Swedish Village into a vibrant central hub for locals and visitors alike. I think the insight we gained from the planners was invaluable. The advice I would give to other small cities is to find the nearest APA chapter and request their help. Once you've received it, follow the road map they provide. Having fresh eyes and decades of experience was amazingly effective.

We love having company. If you are ever in the area, please stop by for an experience you will not obtain anywhere else. Start up a conversation with a local – we're friendly and hospitable. Maybe have a nice glass of award-winning wine from our local winery, see the fully renovated 1923 train station, buy local produce and even Swedish gifts to take home. Plus, you'll have bragging rights as you pose for photos next to one of our many Dale Horses or beneath our giant coffee pot water tower in the park. Come see why Kingsburg made it to the finals of Small Business Revolution and how we're sustaining our momentum.

Jessica Palumbo, Main Street Manager
Frostburg First
Frostburg, MD

From the moment Amanda Brinkman held up a white cue card with Frostburg, MD proudly displayed, an enormous wave of excitement and energy began flowing through our little Mountain City. Within minutes of the Facebook Live announcement of the Top 8 semi-finalists, our phone began ringing off the hook: calls from local business owners, the mayor, residents of neighboring counties. The word spread like wildfire!

Through the #MyFrostburg campaign, people who hold Frostburg dear to their hearts were able to share old photos and stories of days gone by. Some fondly remembered the old trolley cars that used to cart residents up and down Main Street. Others shared memories from TeenTown, a popular hangout spot for youths in the '50s and '60s. Many Frostburg State alumni wrote that they still pine for a local watering hole's "Frostburg famous" chili. Scrolling through the hashtag posts, one thing was clear: people were falling in love with Frostburg, whether for the first or five-hundredth time.

Much of Frostburg's small-town charm lies in its history. As an Appalachian town built and sustained by coal miners and educators, Frostburg has always been resilient, recovering from devastating fires to the loss of industry, and even a damaging tornado. Frostburg has come to view change as a chance for reinvention, an opportunity to instill age-old community values into fresh ventures. In the past two years alone, Frostburg has cut ribbons for over 15 new businesses, while also celebrating 10-, 25-, 30-, and 75-year anniversaries for some of Main Street's staple businesses. This second wave of Main Street business owners allows the older and younger generations to learn from one another. Older generations can offer time-tested

211

advice on small-town business practices, while the younger, more tech-savvy generation gives a fresher perspective on what appeals to millennials – important knowledge in a college town!

This mix of both old and new businesses is a prime example of what Frostburg is all about: people coming together to work toward a common cause. Almost immediately after the nomination announcement, we began holding brainstorming sessions on how we could spread the word about our nomination. Each session saw a growing number of participants with wide and diverse skill sets; attendees included local business owners, representatives from Frostburg State University, non-profit directors, and community members. Through these workshops, we were reminded that our community's greatest asset is its people, and when people come together to complete a task, a revolution will begin.

And a revolution has begun in Frostburg! Our nomination for the Top 8 was like stepping on to an escalator on our journey towards the economic revitalization of our downtown. Business owners are energized and motivated to step up their marketing strategies, and community members and out-of-town visitors alike are more excited than ever to patronize the small businesses on Main Street. In the midst of lively times on Main Street, Frostburg, even greater opportunities can be seen on the path ahead.

Simultaneous to the Small Business Revolution, the City of Frostburg completed a Target Industry Analysis with Site Selection Group, LLC out of Dallas, Texas. The aim of the analysis was to assess regional assets and opportunities to determine industries that are best suited for the region and culture, utilizing the skills of students graduating from programs at the three regional educational institutions: Garrett College, Allegany College of Maryland, and Frostburg State University. In the months since the Small Business Revolution, the City of Frostburg has initiated an effort called Frostburg Forward, using the Strategic Doing framework, bringing together economic development leaders, educators, and marketers to propel our region forward, based on the findings of the target industry analysis.

The Small Business Revolution helped our community realize the wonderful things that can be accomplished when we work together. Frostburg Forward, although regional in nature, is a community based collaborative process that is looking to build upon the strengths of our community to improve our workforce, grow our population, share our history, and encourage entrepreneurs – all which ultimately can strengthen the economy of our Main Street.

Christine Flohr
Director of Tourism, Wabash County, Indiana
2016 Winner Small Business Revolution- Main Street

July 28, 2016

Mr. Lee Schram, CEO
Deluxe Corporation
3680 Victoria St. N
Shoreview, MN 55126

*"Just as ripples spread out when a single pebble is dropped into water,
the actions of individuals can have far-reaching effects."* – **Dalai Lama**

Mr. Schram,

Rarely do pivotal moments occur in a competitive world where the bottom-line drives the actions of Corporate America and employees are measured in ROI percentages. We would be remiss if we failed to pause and recognize how The Small Business Revolution – Main Street project helped change the trajectory of a remote Indiana town that struggles to remain relevant. Like the adage of the pebble and the ripple – a strategic vision to rebrand a 100-year-old company has resulted in revolutionizing an entire city.

There is a common thread that weaves itself seamlessly through the fabric of the SBR project. The common thread is sincerity... so purposefully inserted into every thought and action that centers itself at the core of execution. The thought-leader to toss the pebble into unchartered waters was Amanda Brinkman. The ripple effect of that decision continues to cascade over a movement born from a selfless and successful approach of connecting the consumer with the rebrand of a well-known "check company."

Securing and empowering a team to launch a project 563 miles from headquarters with a multitude of incalculable variables is risky, even for a Fortune 500 Company with a Shark at its heels. So how did a group of

214

executives from Shoreview, MN successfully evoke impactful change in Wabash, Indiana? By building sincere relationships. By listening. By leading. By guiding. By showing empathy. By supporting big ideas and misplaced good intentions.

From the first interaction via the telephone with the team from Flow Nonfiction to professional introductions and handshakes with Amanda, Cameron and Julie, a sincere relationship was formed and so began this small town's quest to be the winner of the Small Business Revolution – Main Street contest. It was their sincere and mindful interactions with the citizens of Wabash that ignited the power of collaboration within an entire community.

As we look into the rearview mirror and evaluate the value of a contest designed to change the conversation about Deluxe's services, we realize that the brilliant minds, kind hearts, and world-class leaders of your corporation have forever changed our minds, our hearts and our leaders. An investment of half a million dollars in goods, services & improvements offers tangible effects of a well-designed strategic marketing initiative, and Wabash will be forever grateful. However, potluck dinners, backyard basketball games, tears, selfies, laughter, growth, friendships and memories cannot be quantified in percentages or dollars and cents. A series of sincere and purposeful decisions made by progressive thought-leaders is how lasting change occurs, a revolution starts, and ripples continue.

On behalf of the Visit Wabash County Board of Directors and Team, it is with sincerity I would like to thank Deluxe Corporation for the $10,000 investment earmarked for this organization in addition to the overwhelming generosity already bestowed upon the City of Wabash. We will be excellent stewards of this gift. It will enable us to advance our mission of marketing Wabash County as a destination to travelers and developers.

With sincere gratitude,

Christine Flohr

Contact Us.

Bill Pezza has been active in government and civic groups on all levels for over forty years. He is an accomplished and engaging motivational speaker and workshop leader with a proven record of success in community planning, volunteer recruitment, goal setting and building public/private partnerships.

Contact Bill at bpezza@comcast.net to explore options to address your civic group or lead your next workshop.